THEN & NOW

THEN & NOW

STEFANIA & DOMINIC PERRING

Macmillan Publishing Company
NEW YORK

Maxwell Macmillan Canada
TORONTO

Maxwell Macmillan International
NEW YORK   OXFORD   SINGAPORE   SYDNEY

A QUARTO BOOK

Macmillan Publishing Company
866 Third Avenue, New York, NY 10022

Maxwell Macmillan Canada, Inc.
1200 Eglinton Avenue East, Suite 200
Don Mills, Ontario M3C 3N1

Macmillan Publishing Company
is part of the Maxwell Communication Group of Companies

Library of Congress Cataloging-in-Publication Data

Perring, Stefania
  Then & now/Stefania and Dominic Perring
      p.   cm.
  ISBN 0-02-599461-1
  1. Civilization, Ancient – Pictorial works. 2. Antiquities – Pictorial
  works. I. Perring, Dominic. II. Title. III. Title: Then and now
CB311.P45 1991   91-3867 CIP
930-dc20

This book was designed and produced by Quarto Publishing plc
The Old Brewery, 6 Blundell Street, London N7 9BH

PROJECT CO-ORDINATOR Laura Sandelson
PICTURE RESEARCH Liz Eddison
RECONSTRUCTIONS Norman Bancroft Hunt
DESIGNER Nicky Chapman
ART DIRECTOR Terry Jeavons

Quarto acknowledges with grateful thanks Professor Brian Fagan's
contribution to the article on Mesa Verde to THEN & NOW.
It also thanks Dr Elizabeth Moore for her help in the preparation of
the material for the Temple of Bayon, Angkor Thom.

Typeset in Great Britain by
Central Southern Typesetters, Eastbourne
Reproduced by Excel Graphic Art, Hong Kong
Printed by Saik Wah Press Pte. Ltd.

10 9 8 7 6 5 4 3 2

CONTENTS

INTRODUCTION

Ruins, of whatever description, always stimulate the imagination. There is something deeply evocative about them; there is also something about them that immediately arouses the curiosity of even the casual observer. Take the mighty temples the ancient Egyptians built in the Nile valley, or the ruins of Pompeii and the cliff dwellings of the Anasazi Indians in the canyons of Mesa Verde, in Colorado. On seeing them, we immediately start to wonder about the lives, or deaths, of the people who built them, not to mention what such people were striving to create in places that, to us, may seem out-of-the-way.

In general terms, these basic speculations hold true, whatever the exact nature or purpose of the ruin or site. They give us a point of contact with the peoples of past times. Sometimes, we find ourselves face-to-face with the echoes of alien cultures, of past worlds that fascinate because of their obvious difference from our own. Or it may be that the attraction lies in what the ruins tell us about the details of daily life – the touches of commonplace domesticity that bridge the gap between past and present, reminding us of our common humanity. Or the appeal may be primarily a romantic one – some ruins may inspire us to dwell on the wonders of a past "golden age," on heroic times that seem more exciting than our own.

In fact, the past is a little of all these things – horrific, mundane and romantic. Above all, however, it is a place of our own invention. Since it cannot exist in any tangible sense – it cannot be touched, measured or experienced – it has to be remembered and imagined. Bridging the gap is the task of archaeologists – their discoveries provide the clues to enable the exercise of reasoned imagination.

In THEN & NOW, we have attempted just such an exercise in considered imagination in trying to rekindle life into some of the world's greatest archaeological monuments. With a little artistic licence – enough anyway to compensate for the fact that the camera can and does lie on matters of perspective – our ruins have been restored to their pristine condition, to appear as they did in their prime.

The sites shown in these pages have been selected for their pull on the imagination. They are the places where the temptation to step back in time is at its strongest. Though it could be argued that there is a slight Western bias in the selection, it has nevertheless proved possible to include a fair representation of the most impressive, evocative and important of the world's great archaeological landmarks.

It is as well to remember, however, that these sites are unlikely to provide much insight into the ordinary lives of past peoples. Most of the places painstakingly reconstructed here are the spectacular products of civilizations at their peak – they are monuments of state, built to glorify and perpetuate a particular ruling system. In most periods, the ordinary people built modest houses from perishable materials – even the Romans built more houses of timber and clay than of brick and stone. Such structures were of such an ephemeral nature that even the most skilled archaeological fieldworkers can find it hard to pick out the slight soil discolorations that are all that is left of their walls and floors.

Far more than the present, the past presents a landscape dominated by the lives of the rich, powerful and famous. Some of the buildings featured in **THEN & NOW** were the work of a particular ruler – examples include the Emperor Hadrian's villa at Tivoli, Jayavarman VII's temple at Angkor and Zoser's pyramid at Saqqara. Others, such as the palace at Knossos and the Tower of London, were the headquarters of a ruling dynasty. In other cases, it was a more abstract and extended concept of government that was represented. Examples of this include not just the public buildings positioned around the main squares of Athens and Rome, but entire capital cities, such as Nimrud, Mohenjo-Daro, Great Zimbabwe and Teotihuacan.

Governments have also always sought divine backing for their rule, so temples and churches feature prominently. The temples of Karnak, Angkor, Nimrud, Teotihuacan, Jerusalem and Athens all served as symbols of state, far exceeding the demands of piety in the ambition and pretension of their design. And, of the sites examined here, Masada, though not built as a monument of state, has become one because of its later contribution to the affirmation of statehood.

THE GREAT CIVILIZATIONS

The time chart (right) shows the civilizations featured in the main part of the book, with their approximate beginning and end dates. The individual sites are listed within the individual bands, with the dates of the reconstructions.

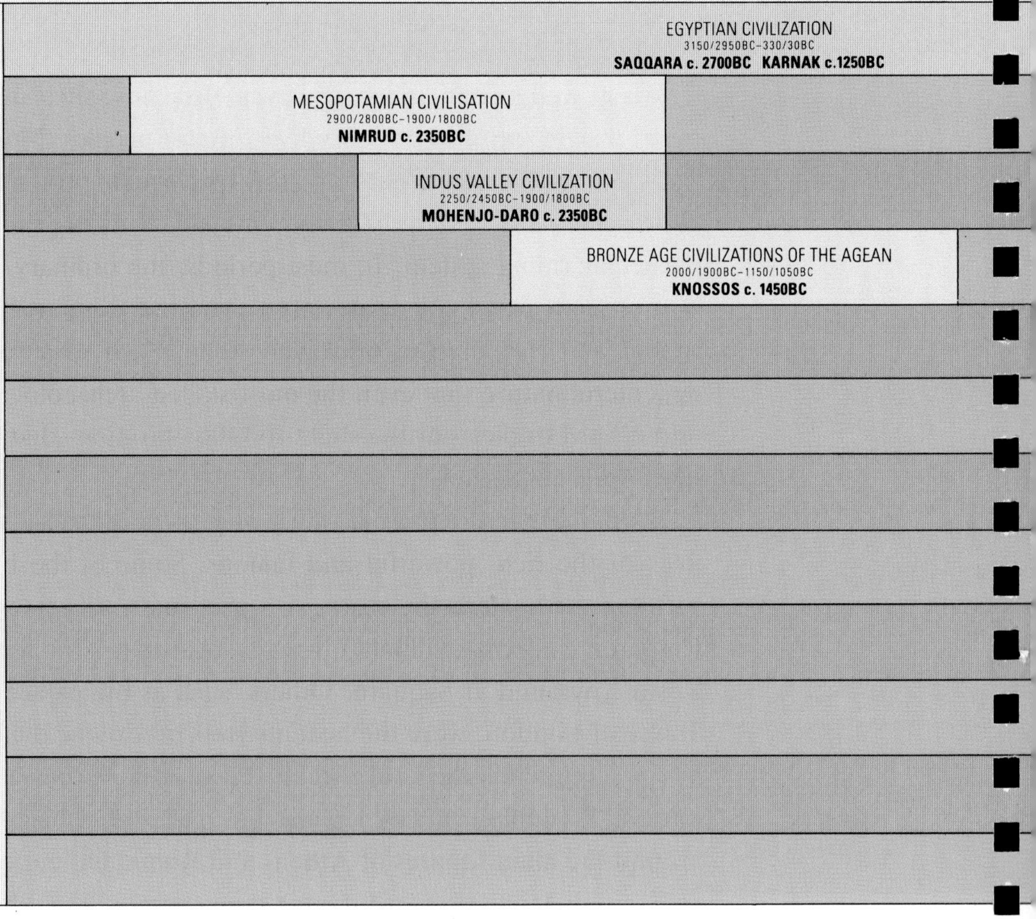

EGYPTIAN CIVILIZATION
3150/2950BC–330/30BC
SAQQARA c. 2700BC   KARNAK c.1250BC

MESOPOTAMIAN CIVILISATION
2900/2800BC–1900/1800BC
NIMRUD c. 2350BC

INDUS VALLEY CIVILIZATION
2250/2450BC–1900/1800BC
MOHENJO-DARO c. 2350BC

BRONZE AGE CIVILIZATIONS OF THE AGEAN
2000/1900BC–1150/1050BC
KNOSSOS c. 1450BC

In other words, there is a surprising consistency in the message conveyed by the world's great archaeological sites. In the final analysis, the needs of man and state have differed little across the passage of time.

One other feature shared by all but a couple of these sites is their eventual failure. Great civilizations, despite their claims to the contrary, are inevitably mortal. And perhaps the most lasting impression gained from prolonged contemplation of these empty ruins is one of transient mortality.

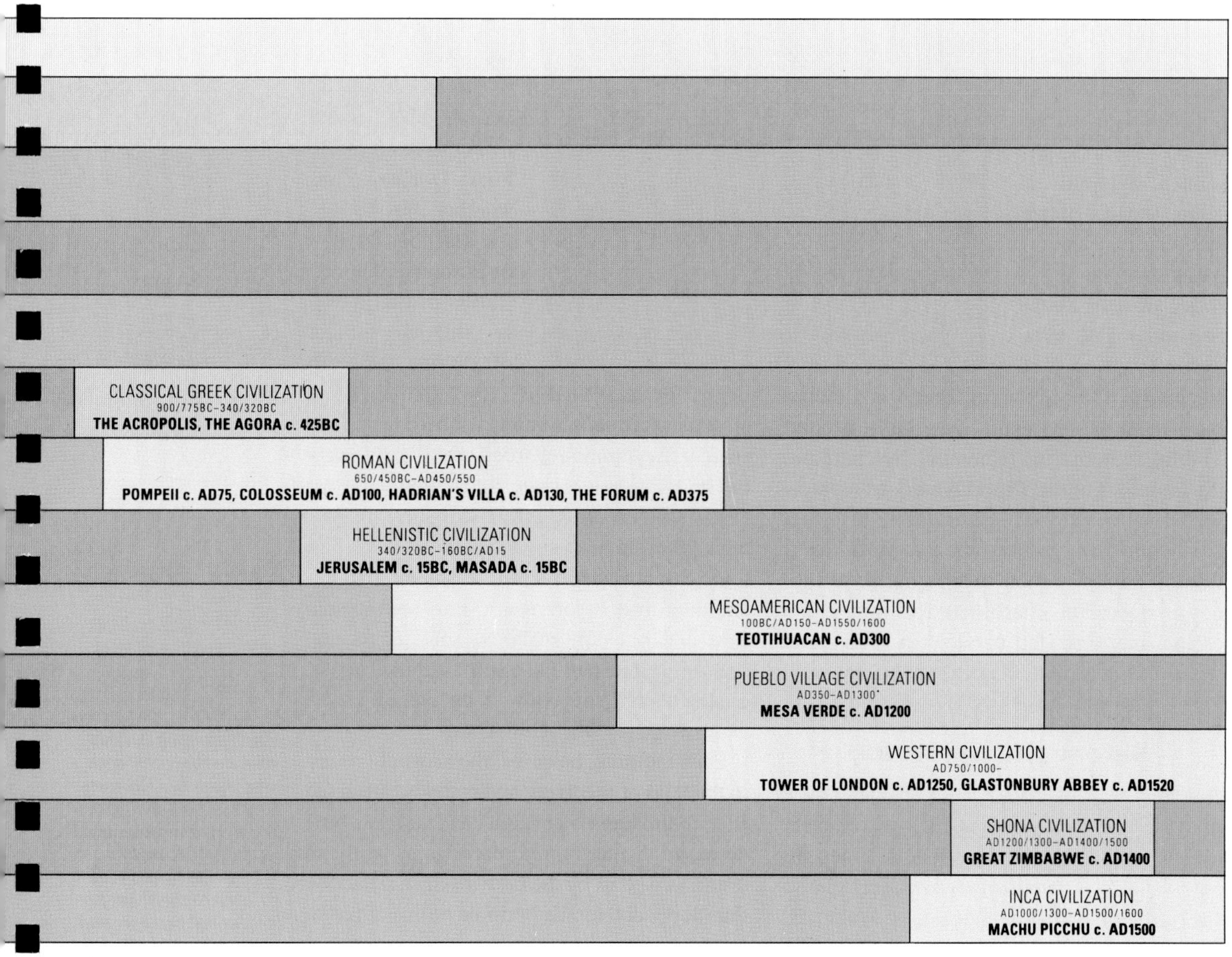

CLASSICAL GREEK CIVILIZATION
900/775BC–340/320BC
THE ACROPOLIS, THE AGORA c. 425BC

ROMAN CIVILIZATION
650/450BC–AD450/550
POMPEII c. AD75, COLOSSEUM c. AD100, HADRIAN'S VILLA c. AD130, THE FORUM c. AD375

HELLENISTIC CIVILIZATION
340/320BC–160BC/AD15
JERUSALEM c. 15BC, MASADA c. 15BC

MESOAMERICAN CIVILIZATION
100BC/AD150–AD1550/1600
TEOTIHUACAN c. AD300

PUEBLO VILLAGE CIVILIZATION
AD350–AD1300
MESA VERDE c. AD1200

WESTERN CIVILIZATION
AD750/1000–
TOWER OF LONDON c. AD1250, GLASTONBURY ABBEY c. AD1520

SHONA CIVILIZATION
AD1200/1300–AD1400/1500
GREAT ZIMBABWE c. AD1400

INCA CIVILIZATION
AD1000/1300–AD1500/1600
MACHU PICCHU c. AD1500

THE STEP PYRAMID

*In the desert sands of ancient Egypt, the first pyramid is
raised to house the body of a mighty Pharaoh*

Narmer (Menes)

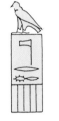

Djoser-Netcherikhe

Sneferu

Khufu (Cheops)

Khafra

Menkaura

Saqqara's so-called step pyramid is a major milestone in the history of human achievement. Not only is it the father of all of Egypt's subsequent pyramids; it is the world's oldest stone-built monument. Dominating a rocky plateau about two miles (3.2 kilometers) west of Memphis, the capital of the newly-united kingdom, the pyramid was built around 2700BC to house the remains of Netcherikhe, the first ruler of the Third Dynasty who, later, was also known as Djoser. Only with his accession to the throne was a powerful, centralized administration strong enough to subdue all opposition established; the construction of the imposing step pyramid in solid stone was thus a logical monument to this powerful king's achievements.

Before the pyramids

Saqqara, probably named after Sokkar, a local god of the dead, was probably a royal cemetery even before Djoser-Netcherikhe founded his new dynasty. This discovery is largely due to the work of British archaeologist Walter B. Emery, who began working on the site in 1935, uncovering 12 huge mastaba tombs – rectangular sun baked mud-brick buildings built along the lines of the houses of the period. All 12 dated from the times of the First Dynasty, but whether they housed the kings themselves or powerful administrators of the period is still a subject of dispute between Egyptologists. What is clear, though these mastaba were subsequently robbed, is that the ancient Egyptians regarded even these early rulers as gods incarnate and equipped their tombs with everything necessary for a comfortable afterlife – even down to lavatories in some cases. Every attempt was made to emulate their lives before death. For them, a man consisted not only of body, soul, name and shadow, but also of *ka*, a spirit double, which, on death, left the body to be judged in the underworld by the God Osiris.

Each morning, however, the *ka* would return to the land of the living and could be attracted back to the tomb by pictures and statues of the deceased dignatory and offerings of food and drink, as well as by the body itself. Eternal life thus depended on the periodic return of the *ka* to the mummified corpse.

Each pharaoh had his own hieroglyphic seal, or cartouche. The ones (above) are those of the great pyramid-builders of the Old Kingdom. The statue (inset) is of Djoser-Netcherikhe, for whom the step pyramid was built.

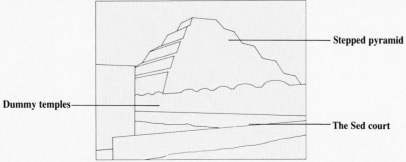

Stepped pyramid

Dummy temples

The Sed court

Imhotep – the royal builder

The step pyramid itself was the work of Imhotep, Djoser-Netcherikhe's chancellor. Later generations credited him with the invention of stone building and revered him as an architect, astronomer, mathematician, writer and doctor – in Greek times, he was deified as a patron god of medicine. From the start, Imhotep chose stone as his building medium and, even though his design started life as another mastaba, he seized on the chance of developing his ideas during the process of construction. The step pyramid was the final result.

The original mastaba, with its central granite-lined burial chamber and vertical access shaft, became the foundations for the eventual pyramid. The mastaba's sides were around 200ft (62.5 meters) in length; its overall height was 26 feet (7.9 meters). Imhotep proceeded to set three more mastaba blocks on top of it to form a four-step pyramid and the whole base was then enlarged westward and northward to allow the final two steps to be added. When building was finally completed, the whole exterior was faced with a smooth outer cladding of limestone.

While work was proceeding on the pyramid, a warren of underground galleries and passageways were built around the burial chamber, which, after the king's coffin had been laid to rest there, was sealed with a granite plug. The walls of the passages leading away from the chamber were decorated with relief carvings of the king, plus hieroglyphs recording his name. A row of 11 further vertical shafts was also sunk on the eastern face of the pyramid, descending 110 feet (33.5 meters) from its lowest step to a further series of passageways. The remains found in them suggest that they were used as burial chambers for members of the royal family. Two alabaster sarcophagi

THE PYRAMID COMPLEX

The architect Imhotep's work did not stop with the step pyramid (1). The complex he created around it included the Sed court (2), where royal public festivals were held, a southern tomb (3), which may have been a cenotaph and the Houses of the North (4) and South (5). The complex was surrounded by a wall, with one colonnade entrance (6) and several false doors (7).

As the pyramid grew, a network of passages and shafts (1) was created around the central burial chamber (2). Additions included the mortuary complex (3) and serdab (4).

The earliest surviving complete mummy (above left) comes from the tomb of Nefer, also at Saqqara. Imhotep (above right) was the royal chancellor and the step pyramid's inspired architect.

were also found, one of which contained the remains of an eight-year-old boy resting in a coffin made of six layers of wood — the oldest plywood in the world. Another shaft led to a gallery stacked high with 40,000 polished stone vessels, many of which were made of alabaster. They included cups, goblets, bowls, dishes and plates.

Outside the pyramid

The step pyramid was positioned within a large walled precinct, some 1790 feet (545 meters) by 910 feet (270 meters). It housed various stone buildings, many of which have yet to be fully uncovered and excavated. On the north side of the pyramid itself was a mortuary temple, from which an entrance tunnel led down to the burial chamber and to which the priests brought their daily offerings of food and drink. The temple's design in itself is unusual, since everything, from courts and rooms down to columns, is duplicated. This is thought to symbolize the fact that royal authority extended over both Lower and Upper Egypt.

Other buildings in the precinct may have been copied from the king's palace of Memphis. The most important of them is the Sed court. The barrel-vaulted temples that surround it were for decorative and symbolic effect only, their facades concealing solid stone. On the top of each of the four supporting columns of each facade were carved large round holes. These probably held flagpoles, which might have carried symbols representing various Egyptian deities, or banners representing the different political areas, or *nomes*, of Upper and Lower Egypt.

The Sed festival

The area in front of the chapels was where the Sed festival was celebrated, a ceremony that originated as a physical test of the king's fitness to govern Egypt. He did this by running around a set course for each *nome* area. On its successful completion, his coronation was re-enacted, the crowns and ceremonial regalia of office being presented to him as he sat on a dais. Originally, no doubt, success or failure in the test was a matter of life and death — in ancient Egyptian, *sed* itself means "to slay", or "to slaughter." By this time, however, the occasion had become a ceremonial jubilee, in which the king's role as guarantor of the unity and continuity of the state was commemorated.

Ceremonies symbolizing royal renewal may also have made use of another structure within the precinct, known as the southern tomb. This tall building, topped with a decorative frieze of stone cobras, contained two rooms and a concealed subterranean chamber. A small gallery was decorated with reliefs of Djoser-Netcherikhe actually celebrating the Sed festival. Because of its dramatic similarity in layout to that of the main pyramid itself, it is possible that the tomb was a cenotaph.

The pyramid's failure

The step pyramid itself was comprehensively despoiled in antiquity, though excavations in 1934 located part of a mummified foot, which was probably the king's. And even today, there is one spectacle that brings this long-dead ruler vividly back to life. In 1924, Cecil Firth, another British archaeologist, uncovered a small chamber by the entrance to the mortuary chapel. This is known as the Serdab (*serdab* is Arabic for "cellar"). Looking through the two small holes drilled through its stone wall at eye level, he discovered a life-size statue of Djoser-Neterikhe himself. Though the original is now in the Cairo Museum, a duplicate now stands in its place.

THE TEMPLE OF KARNAK

*A colossal temple built on the banks of the Nile to honor
Amun-Re, Egypt's all-powerful ruler of the gods*

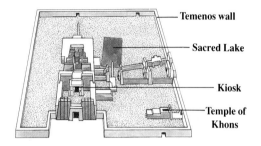

Temenos wall

Sacred Lake

Kiosk

Temple of Khons

One of the most celebrated of the colossal temples built by the ancient Egyptians, Karnak, on the banks of the Nile on the northern edge of the town of Luxor, was a fitting center for the worship of Amun-Re, the all-powerful king of the gods. Building started here at some time between 1500BC and 1350BC; every ruler of Egypt from the start of the New Kingdom onward added to the temple, the result being a vast complex covering five acres (two hectares). Religious and other beliefs influenced temple planning. For example they were built as copies of a legendary first temple, where life was supposed to have emerged from the sea. Its appearance was described in sacred texts, which thus became the basis for all subsequent Egyptian temple construction.

The original temple at Karnak was soon

The plan (above) reveals the scale of the Karnak complex. From it, a sphinx-lined route led to the nearby Temple of Mut, built to honor the wife of Amun-Re. The remains of his temple (right) are seen mirrored in the sacred lake, where his priests bathed daily to purify themselves.

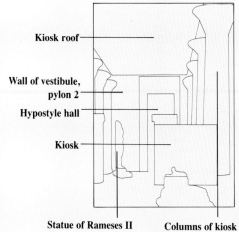

Kiosk roof

Wall of vestibule,
pylon 2

Hypostyle hall

Kiosk

Statue of Rameses II   Columns of kiosk

submerged in a whelter of later additions and extensions. As a consequence, the inner sanctuary is now approached along a processional way through a sequence of six monumental gateways, known as pylons, from the Greek for "doorway." These originally stood over 100 feet (30.5 meters) high. The front of the temple is approached via an avenue, which linked the Karnak complex with that of nearby Luxor.

The hypostyle hall and beyond

The second of these gateways led into the famous multi-columned hypostyle hall, the subject of the reconstruction here. A veritable forest of columns dominates the interior, the central ones flanking the processional way with a further 122 columns arranged in seven rows on either side.

The hall was a dark and secret place, lit only by small clerestory windows high above the columns. Acess was restricted to the king and his priests. Work on it was started by Rameses I and completed by Seti I, though the credit for it was later taken by Rameses II. The names of these kings are carved in cartouches set on the central columns, as are records of their military campaigns.

Worshipping Amun-Re

Beyond lay Karnak's third gateway, built by Amenhotep III, who ordered it to be inlaid in gold and silver, though no trace of this survives today. Progressing through the fourth and fifth pylons, the processional route finally reached Karnak's sanctuary. This was the heart of the temple, its highest and darkest place. The present pink granite structure was added by Philip Arrhidaeus, the brother of Alexander the Great, in around 330BC. Inside

Rameses II (far left) still dominates the temple he took the credit for creating, though work on it started earlier. In the wall-painting (left) he kneels before Amun-Re in the presence of his father Seti I, the moon goddess Khonsu and the mother goddess Mut.

THE PEOPLE AND THE TEMPLE

Though religion was a dominant factor in daily life, the people normally had little direct contact with the temple. They were never allowed to penetrate beyond the front courtyard, the interior being the preserve of the pharaoh and the priests. Nevertheless, vast numbers of them worked for Karnak; a papyrus records that, around 1150BC, 81,322 men were employed.

A man ploughing (below). Karnak owned around 400,000 cattle, sheep and other livestock.

A woman carries a tray of cakes on her head to market or the temple (right).

was a stone dais on which Amun-Re's ceremonial boat was placed, and a shrine, which contained a statue of the god. Temple life revolved around the veneration of this statue by the high priest or king.

To the right of the Festival Hall, built by Tuthmosis III to commemorate his victories and situated across the courtyard behind the sanctuary, was the sacred lake, where, three times a day, the priests would purify themselves. As the Greek historian Herodotus records, cleanliness was a major priestly concern; in addition to continually washing themselves and their white linen gowns, the priests, he reported, also shaved themselves all over every other day.

The god and the people

On major feast days, the customary rituals were modified. The statue of Amun-Re was placed in the cabin of his gilded ceremonial boat, which was carried shoulder high around the perimeter walls of the temple. On these occasions, the god's worshippers could also ask questions of him. To each question, there were two possible answers — yes or no. Scribes wrote the questions on sherds of pottery or stone and these were then laid out on either side of the processional path. As the boat swayed past, it would tilt in favor of one side or the other, so indicating which was correct.

A lasting impact

Herodotus aptly commented that "the Egyptians are religious to excess, beyond any other nation in the world" — and their massive temples confirm the point. Even today, the impact of Karnak can be overwhelming. Small wonder, then, that the great temple here still retains its magic and mystery, taking even the casual spectator back to the days of its glory.

NIMRUD

*The capital of the mighty Assyrian empire carved out with
fire and sword across the ancient Middle East*

On the left bank of the river Tigris in Northern Mesopotamia (modern Iraq) stands a great mound. This is the remains of the ancient Assyrian capital of Nimrud, once the center of a mighty empire that dominated the Middle Eastern world in Old Testament times. Indeed, though the site was known to the Assyrians as Kalhu — the Calah mentioned in the Book of Genesis — it is better known by its Arabic name of Nimrud, after the Biblical hero Nimrod.

The empire that was ruled from here was built by force of arms, reaching its greatest extent in the first half of the 8th century BC. Maintaining control of it kept the formidable Assyrian army constantly at war — its troops winning a deserved reputation as fierce and bloody warriors. Nor were the Assyrian emperors less for-

The great mound (above) is all that remains of Nimrud today, but in the 8th century BC it was a different story. This imaginative lithograph shows the city's royal palaces as they might have appeared in their heyday. Note, too, the massive ziggurat, which stood next to the temple of Ninurta, the Assyrian god of battle and Nimrud's patron deity.

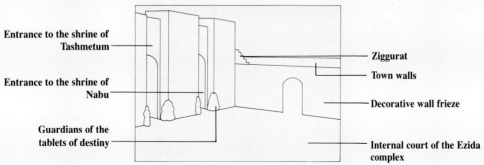

Entrance to the shrine of Tashmetum

Entrance to the shrine of Nabu

Guardians of the tablets of destiny

Ziggurat

Town walls

Decorative wall frieze

Internal court of the Ezida complex

midable. One of the most notable was Assur-nasir-apli, who ruled the empire from 883BC to 859BC. It was Assur-nasir-apli who moved the capital from Assur to Nimrud, where it remained until the end of the 8th century BC, when the center of government shifted first to Korsabad and subsequently to Nineveh.

Nimrud's rediscovery

The subsequent rediscovery of Nimrud did not take place until the 19th century, when the growing European fascination with the

The Black Obelisk (left) is decorated with scenes celebrating the achievements of Shalmanassar III, including the surrender to him of Jehu, the ruler of Israel, in 841BC. Other details include vanquished peoples bearing tribute and columns of camels and other beasts of burden carrying gifts to him. The top is in the form of a ziggurat.

DECORATIVE BOOTY AND TRIBUTE

Excavations at Nimrud have uncovered tens of thousands of delicately carved ivory fragments, which the Assyrians had used to decorate their furniture, including tables and chairs. As well as native ivories, many, like the ones shown here, were imported from the cities of Syria, Palestine and Phoenicia — either taken as booty or given as tribute.

This ivory is decorated with paste inlay. The regional style shows that it was imported, rather than being the work of Assyrian craftsmen.

The skilled craftsmanship of the ivory carvers, down to the close attention they paid to intricate decorative detail, can be seen clearly in this fragment.

This plaque, dating from the 8th to 9th centuries BC, depicts a fabulous mythological winged beast.

These dancing women possibly were originally ornaments on a circular box, or dish stand.

archaeology of the Biblical lands led to the first excavations on the site. These took place in 1845 under the direction of the early British archaeologist Austen Layard. It was the success of his investigations, including the discovery of the famous black obelisk of Shalmaneser III, that inspired the later, more comprehensive research carried out on the site by another major British archaeologist, Max Mallowan. The second husband of the crime writer Dame Agatha Christie, Mallowan directed excavations at Nimrud between 1949 and 1963.

Among Mallowan's discoveries was the splendid six-acre (2.4-hectare) palace of Assurnasirapli II, with its spectacular glazed brick gateways flanked by giant winged beasts. A stone stele (an engraved pillar) found outside the main entrance graphically catalogued the royal achievements — these included military conquests, canal building, skills in hunting and plant collecting — as well as the wonders of the palace Assur-Nasir-apli had had constructed. From it, we learn that the palace included seven suites of rooms, each decorated with a different type of wood, the woods used being box, mulberry, cedar, cypress, pistachio, tamarask and poplar. It also describes the magnificent banquet that was held in 879BC to celebrate the palace's completion.

Expansion and prosperity

Successive kings left their own mark on the expanding capital and, ultimately, palaces, temples, administrative buildings and two-storied mud brick town houses filled the 884-acre (357.7-hectare) site enclosed by the city walls. Surviving inscriptions tell us about the bazaars and markets that were once situated here, as well as referring to the fullers, millers, smiths, carpenters and weavers who made their

living in what might almost be termed the industrial quarters of the city.

One of the main landmarks of this period of prosperity was the so-called Ezida, a courtyard complex that housed the temple of Nabu, the god of writing, destiny and the arts. When the other gods gathered to decide what would happen in the future, it was Nabu's task to record their decisions on clay tablets.

Nabu's sanctuary faced onto the courtyard, its door being guarded by life-sized statues of his attendants holding boxes. These contained the tablets of destiny. An adjacent sanctuary was dedicated to his wife, Tashmetum. In the same complex, under Nabu's protection, were housed the principal archives of the city, along with a scriptorium where scribes worked on the documents recording the temple's properties and goods.

Recording religious beliefs

Excavations here have recovered hundreds of clay tablets, inscribed with cuneiform writing. On decipherment, some were found to record historical and medical matters, but the majority

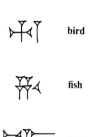

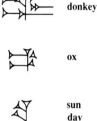

	bird
	fish
	donkey
	ox
	sun day

The Assyrians were careful record-keepers; Nimrud had its state archives, plus a scriptorium for its scribes. The brick here records the name, titles and achievements of Shalmaneser III, including his building of the temple "in the city of Calah."

were religious texts. Some of the superstitions recorded seem very strange to modern eyes, as do some of the medical texts. Nevertheless, there is no doubting the Assyrian respect for scholarship.

Swift collapse

Despite its prosperity and achievement, the Assyrian empire was always difficult to hold together — records show that many cities had to be conquered and reconquered several times over — and its eventual collapse was remarkably swift. Between 630BC and 605BC, Assyria fell victim first to internal strife and then to its neighbors.

Nimrud itself, although no longer the Assyrian capital, was a victim of this collapse. It was sacked and destroyed by a coalition led by the Babylonians in 614BC; the floors found in the upper levels of the excavations there are covered by layers of ashes and debris, the legacy of this disaster. By the end of the 7th century, Babylon had triumphed and the Babylonian ruler Nebuchadnezzar was the master of the whole of Mesopotamia.

THE SECOND TEMPLE

A temple built by the Jews in their capital to celebrate their role as the "chosen people" of the one true God

Jerusalem is one of the world's oldest cities. It is also one of its holiest — a place of pilgrimage for Jew, Christian and Muslim alike. One of its most sacred sites is the mosque of the Dome of the Rock, built in AD631, which is revered not just in itself, but for what lies beneath it. Here are buried the remains of a series of great temples, which once housed the Ark of the Covenant.

It is highly unlikely that archaeologists will ever be given the opportunity to excavate the site. It is far too holy for such a disturbance. Our knowledge of the temples, therefore, comes from the ancient texts that describe them. Fortunately, the Bible exists as a source, plus the writings of the Jewish historian Josephus, which date from the 1st century AD.

The tablets of the law

The site on which the Dome of the Rock stands still dominates modern Jerusalem. It became the city's religious center from at least the 10th century BC, when Solomon, the greatest of the ancient rulers of Israel, built his fabled stone temple here. At its heart, in a gilded and richly carved room that only the High Priest could enter — and then only on one day of the year — stood the Ark of the Covenant. This gilded chest, the most sacred symbol of God's acknowledgment of the Hebrews as the "chosen people," was made by the prophet Moses to hold the two stone tablets on which

These gold coins (far left), minted in Jerusalem at the time of Herod Agrippa, the last Jewish ruler of Judea, carry a view of the sacred second temple. The temple, however, did not long survive his death, being razed to the ground by the Romans in AD 70. This modern model (left) shows how imposing the temple complex must have been in its heyday.

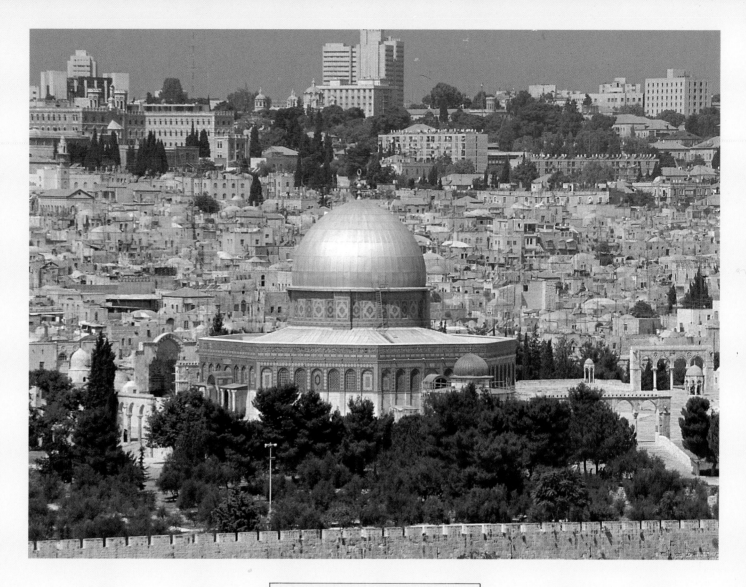

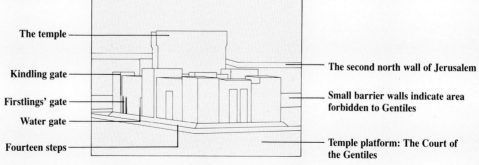

The temple —

Kindling gate —

Firstlings' gate —

Water gate —

Fourteen steps —

— The second north wall of Jerusalem

— Small barrier walls indicate area
forbidden to Gentiles

— Temple platform: The Court of
the Gentiles

were inscribed the laws God had given to the Jews. These had been carried from Mount Sinai to the Promised Land.

The Bible gives us some idea of how splendid Solomon's temple must have been (1 Kings 6), but, like his kingdom, it was not destined to last. When Nebuchadnezzar, ruler of neighboring Babylonia, stormed the city in 586BC, the temple was looted and then destroyed along with the rest of the city. The Jews themselves were marched into their long years of exile and captivity in Babylon. The site was left desolate for some 50 years.

Rebuilding the temple

The Jewish captivity was brought to an end when Cyrus the Great, ruler of Persia and conqueror of Assyria, allowed them to return to Palestine. Between 538 and 513BC, the temple was rebuilt by Zerubbabel, the governor appointed by the Persians. At the dedication ceremony, 100 bullocks, 200 rams, 400 lambs and 12 he-goats — one for each of the tribes of Israel — were sacrificed and all the treasures that could be recovered from Babylon ceremoneously restored. However, it seems that the Ark of the Covenant had been completely destroyed.

In 20BC, however, ambition and power politics took a hand in the temple's destiny. In that year, a massive rebuilding scheme started, ordered by Herod the Great, friend to Rome and ruler of what was now called Judea. Even though Herod's kingdom had been enlarged by the Emperor Augustus, his links with Rome earned him considerable unpopularity among the Jews and the ambitious plans for the temple were part of his attempts to win over his restless subjects.

Herod refashioned the temple in the Hellenistic style. It took only 18 months to finish the

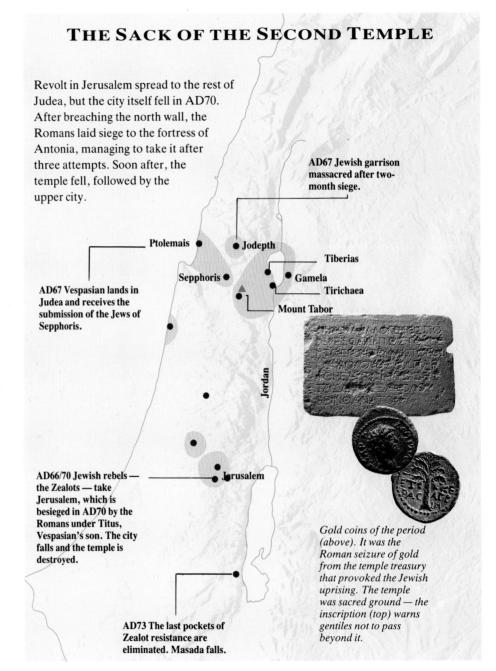

THE SACK OF THE SECOND TEMPLE

Revolt in Jerusalem spread to the rest of Judea, but the city itself fell in AD70. After breaching the north wall, the Romans laid siege to the fortress of Antonia, managing to take it after three attempts. Soon after, the temple fell, followed by the upper city.

AD67 Jewish garrison massacred after two-month siege.

Ptolemais

Jodepth

Tiberias

Sepphoris

Gamela

Tirichaea

AD67 Vespasian lands in Judea and receives the submission of the Jews of Sepphoris.

Mount Tabor

Jordan

AD66/70 Jewish rebels — the Zealots — take Jerusalem, which is besieged in AD70 by the Romans under Titus, Vespasian's son. The city falls and the temple is destroyed.

Jerusalem

Gold coins of the period (above). It was the Roman seizure of gold from the temple treasury that provoked the Jewish uprising. The temple was sacred ground — the inscription (top) warns gentiles not to pass beyond it.

AD73 The last pockets of Zealot resistance are eliminated. Masada falls.

main parts of the project, though, according to Josephus, it was not completed until AD62 to 64. For it, Herod utilized the services of a team of 1000 priests specially trained as masons — this was necessary because only priests were allowed to tread the consecrated ground. The temple platform, which covers an area of some 35 acres (14 hectares), still survives, as does the western section of the massive enclosure walls — some 15 feet (4.5 meters) thick and built of enormous stones up to 30 feet (9.1 meters) long. This is the celebrated Wailing Wall of modern Judaism.

From the eastern side of the platform there was a sheer drop into the valley below; the southeast corner of the precinct was the probable location of the temple pinnacle referred to in Satan's temptation of Christ (Matthew 4). Gates on all sides led to the platform. The two entrances to the south were approached via flights of stairs between which were positioned baths for ritual purification. On the western side, one of the gates was reached by a viaduct from the upper city.

The Court of the Gentiles

Inside the walls, surrounding the temple itself, was the Court of the Gentiles – "gentile" is the name given by the Jews to anyone who is non-Jewish. This was a public space, enclosed by white marble colonnades. Money changers and livestock merchants, selling animals such as oxen, sheep and doves for sacrifice at the temple, sat beneath the porticoes. The livestock merchants were particularly rapacious; the prices of birds, the traditional offering of the poor, reached such levels that the priests were compelled to impose price limits.

The Court of the Gentiles was separated from the sacred areas immediately around the temple by a balustrade, inscriptions in Latin

An orthodox Israeli of today prays at the Wailing Wall (above). Although, following the sack of Jerusalem, the temple and its high priesthood vanished for ever, the Jews survived the centuries of dispersion and persecution that followed.

and Greek warning gentiles that entrance was forbidden and trespass was punishable by death. From there, a short flight of stairs led to the ten entrances to the inner courts, decorated in silver and gold. To the east was the Court of the Women, beyond which women were not allowed to proceed. From there yet another stairway led to the bronze doors of the Court of Israel. Here, men could watch the sacrifices and religious ceremonies being carried out in the Court of the Priests.

The inner sanctum

The 23-foot-high (seven meters) sacrificial altar stood immediately in front of the temple proper. Here, priests sacrificed animals and burned plants and incense to God. Only priests were allowed to perform this rite.

The temple itself was built of white marble, clad in shimmering gold. Originally, Herod had also placed a gold eagle above its door — perhaps in imitation of a Greco-Roman temple pediment — but this profane image so offended Jewish sensibilities that an angry mob tore it down and destroyed it. Inside were the holiest of Jewish treasures, the most important of which was the menorah, the great seven-branched candelabra made by Moses, along with the golden table on which 12 loaves of bread were ceremoniously placed on the Jewish sabbath. In an inner room, the holy of holies, a block of marble stood in the place of the lost Ark of the Covenant.

The final fall

When the last Herod — Herod Agrippa — died in AD44, the uneasy relationship between Romans and Jews finally broke down. Herod was replaced by a series of corrupt Roman procurators, one of whom, Florus, finally provoked a full-scale rising through his brutal suppression of a riot that followed his seizure of gold from the temple treasury in AD64. The Romans reacted ruthlessly and, in AD68, Vespasian, commander of the legions in the east, marched on Jerusalem. Recalled to Rome to succeed the Emperor Nero, he left his son, Titus, in charge of the resulting siege.

A few days before Passover in AD70, Titus laid siege to the city. Although the defenders fought with great courage, the temple precincts were eventually stormed five months later. According to tradition, this took place on 9 Av, the anniversary of the fall of the first temple to the Babylonians. Rome had triumphed and the temple was razed.

MASADA

Deep in the Judean desert, determined Zealot rebels resist the might of Rome . . . and then commit mass suicide, rather than surrender

Set on a stunning rocky outcrop above the western shores of the Dead Sea, the ancient mountain-top fortress of Masada, with its sheer sides dropping away for some 1300 feet (396 meters), has an honored place in Jewish history. Here, in AD73, the last of the Zealots, who had held out for two years in the face of a Roman siege, committed suicide rather than face defeat and enslavement — a story described in detail by the contemporary Jewish historian Josephus in his book *The Jewish War*.

The Romans brought their siege artillery into play at Masada, but it made little impact on the citadel's solid man-made and natural defences. The ballista (above) threw stones weighing up to 6lbs (2.7kg).

Masada and Herod the Great

According to Josephus, Masada was first fortified by Alexander Jannaeus sometime between 113 and 76BC, but the fortifications as they exist today are largely the work of Herod the Great, who built them around 40BC. Masada was no ordinary fort, however. As a young man, Herod himself had been forced to take refuge there during a period of bitter civil war, so his building program was designed not just to strengthen the existing defenses, but to provide the king and his family with a luxurious palace in which to take refuge in times of trouble.

The fortress itself was surrounded by a great double wall, reinforced by a series of towers. Within these confines, Herod built barracks for a strong garrison, vast storerooms and a chain of enormous water cisterns — everything necessary, in fact, to withstand even a prolonged siege successfully. He also built two great palaces. One, richly ornamented in the Hellenistic style, extended across three hanging terraces right at the northern tip of the plateau — hence its name, the Hanging Palace. This is the subject of the reconstruction. The other was set on the highest part of Masada and contained administrative, residential and reception suites set around a series of courtyards. The building also possessed its own storerooms, which contained a variety of

The reconstruction (right) shows Herod's famous and aptly-named three-tiered Hanging Palace, nestling among the rocks. The photograph (below) shows how impregnable Masada must have seemed to its Zealot garrison and their Roman attackers. Remains of the Roman siege ramp can be seen on the right.

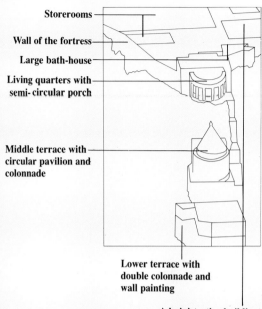

Storerooms

Wall of the fortress

Large bath-house

Living quarters with
semi- circular porch

Middle terrace with
circular pavilion and
colonnade

Lower terrace with
double colonnade and
wall painting

Administrative buildings

sophisticated and expensive goods not to be found in the public stores — at least so it would seem from the fragments of small pottery oil jugs and flasks archaeologists have found here. At the time of the Roman siege, these contained dry figs, a nutritious food that takes up little storage space.

Herod's private bath has also been rediscovered, with its series of hot and cold rooms, plunge baths and mosaic floors. Elsewhere, there were public baths and a swimming pool.

Romans and Zealots

Masada did not remain under Jewish control. Herod died in 4BC and in AD6 a Roman garrison took control of the fortress when direct rule was imposed on Judea, the country becoming an imperial province. In AD66, however, a band of rebel Zealots, led by Eleazer ben Ya'ir, launched a surprise attack on the fortress and massacred its garrison. The Zealots promptly occupied the site, establishing their homes in the fortress walls.

The austere Zealots had no need to Herodian luxury, so what they built at Masada was modest in scale. They cannibalized parts of the columns of the Hanging Palace for use in the construction of their sacred baths and synagogue; they also used its elegant timber pavements as firewood. Evidence of their presence has been found scattered across the site — notably everyday objects, such as a pair of child's sandals, toiletries, lamps and pots, along with bows and arrows and coins of the period. The Zealots used coins as tokens to ensure fair distribution of goods and services.

With the destruction of Jerusalem in AD70, Masada became one of the last pockets of Zealot resistance in Judea. Determined to crush this, the 15,000-strong Roman Tenth Legion marched on the fortress and a siege

lasting for almost two years ensued. The Zealot garrison, including women and children as well as men, is thought to have numbered around 1000.

The task facing the Romans was formidable. The storerooms of the fortress were full, while the besieging Romans depended on a long and treacherous supply line — even water for the troops had to be brought across the surrounding desert. The defences, too, seemed impregnable. Eventually, Flavius Silva, the governor of the province, realized that it would be impossible for his troops to take Masada simply by isolating it and starving the Zealots into submission. There was no alternative to a full-scale assault.

The Romans had already ringed Masada with a chain of fortified camps, linking these with a six-foot-thick (1.8 meters) siege wall. This wall was 3,800 yards (4,374 meters) long, with towers positioned at 80 yard (24 meter) to 100 yards (30 meter) intervals. The next step was to build a huge ramp up which a giant battering ram could be hauled to breach the defenses. This took the Romans a further seven months. Then the onslaught began.

Mass suicide at Masada

The Zealots resisted successfully at first. Then, a wood-revetted part of the stone rampart caught fire, weakened and collapsed. As the Romans regrouped for their final attack, the Zealots assembled to consider their fate.

There was no chance of flight — nor could any mercy be expected from their Roman foes. The grim answer was mass suicide. Josephus vividly describes the tragic arguments and events of that fateful night: "Miserable men indeed were they! Whose distress forced them to slay their own wives and childen with their own hands, as the lightest of the evils that

A STRUGGLE TO

From AD66, when a Zealot force massacred Masada's Roman garrison, to AD73, when the citadel finally fell to the besieging Tenth Lregion, the Jewish rebels at Masada continued to fight for their beliefs. They left many traces of their occupancy behind them; this ended in grim tragedy, when almost all the Zealots killed themselves rather than face the humiliation of defeat and surrender. The Romans found a room of corpses on entering the burning palace — 960 men, women and children lay huddled together in death.

These bronze trinkets — a fibula (left), buckles (center), key (bottom right) and knob (top right) — were found in one of the 110 rooms of the casemate walls.

Leather sandals, found near a woman's skeleton on the pool steps look modern.

THE DEATH – AND A MOVING LEGACY

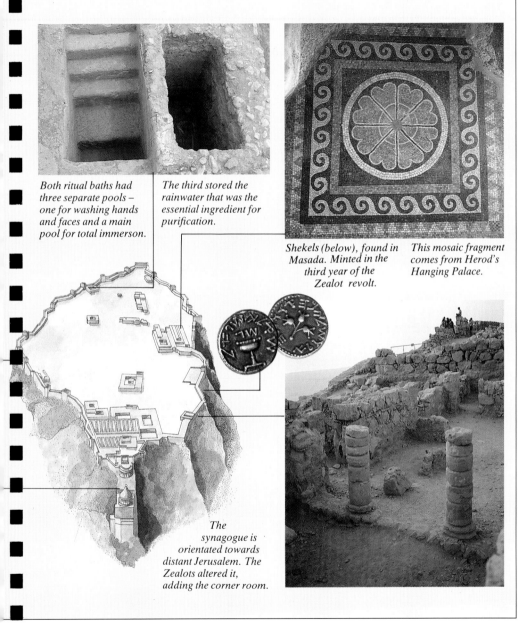

Both ritual baths had three separate pools – one for washing hands and faces and a main pool for total immerson.

The third stored the rainwater that was the essential ingredient for purification.

Shekels (below), found in Masada. Minted in the third year of the Zealot revolt.

This mosaic fragment comes from Herod's Hanging Palace.

The synagogue is orientated towards distant Jerusalem. The Zealots altered it, adding the corner room.

were before them. So not being able to bear the grief they were under for what they had done any longer and esteeming it an injury to those they had slain to live even the shortest space of time after them, they presently laid all they had in a heap and set fire to it. They then chose ten men by lot out of them to slay all the rest, every one of whom laid himself down by his wife and children on the ground and threw his arms about them, and they offered their necks to the stroke of those who executed that melancholy office; and when these ten had, without fear, slain them all, they made the same rule for casting lots for themselves, that he whose lot it was should first kill the other nine, and after all, should kill himself."

The archaeological evidence supports this account. *Ostraka* (sherds of pottery) found on the site, have names painted on them, including that of Eleazer ben Ya'ir himself.

The grim aftermath

The following morning, the Romans moved to the assault, but, instead of the fierce resistance they expected, they met with a terrible silence. Some of Masada's buildings were still on fire, but there were no signs of the Zealots. Recovering from their initial surprise, the legionnaires called out and eventually two women and five small children emerged from the underground caverns. They explained that they were Masada's only survivors. Entering the burning palace, the Romans found grim confirmation of this sorry tale.

This was not the end of the story. A Roman garrison was reestablished at Masada and held the fortress for at least the next 40 years. In the 5th or 6th centuries AD, a colony of Byzantine monks occupied the ruins. And today Masada is an Israeli national shrine,

THE PALACE OF KNOSSOS

The center of the brilliant Minoan civilization that dominated the world of the ancient Agean

Linear B tablets (below), found at Knossos, were used by the Minoans to tally a variety of foodstuffs and imported goods as they passed through the palace stores.

ti — ri — po — de

Linear B came into use in Minoan Crete as the Myceneans increased their influence. It replaced the earlier Linear A, which is still undeciphered. The example here show how Linear B was decoded word-for-word, working through its links with ancient Cypriot.

There is frequently a fine dividing line between where legend ends and history begins; indeed, the two are sometimes totally inter-related. As far as ancient Europe is concerned, this is certainly true of the Greek Bronze Age — the era described so brilliantly by the epic poet Homer and, archaeologically, brought back to life by the discoveries that have been made at Troy, Mycenae and Knossos. This last was Homer's "mighty city . . . wherein Minos ruled;" historically, it has been proved to be one of the centers of the flourishing Minoan civilization, which reached the height of its power and influence during the second millenium BC.

Archaeology and legend

Knossos was the most important of a series of elaborate palaces, around which the Minoan civilization was organized. These Minoans, it is thought, were descendants of the original inhabitants of Crete, who perhaps migrated to the island from somewhere in the Middle East, though the view that they were refugees fleeing from turmoil in Old Kingdom Egypt is now exploded.

What is certain is that the site at Knossos was occupied in Neolithic times, remains of mudbrick and wooden houses dating from as early as 6000 BC having been discovered there in the lowest levels of archaeological excavation. These excavations started at Knossos in

The northern entrance to the palace. The gate to the right led to the road to the port – the Minoans were the first people in the world to build paved roads. The two-storied building to the left was probably a dining hall.

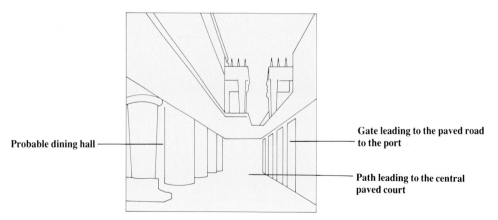

Probable dining hall ─

Gate leading to the paved road to the port

Path leading to the central paved court

the late 19th century and have continued there at intervals ever since, the bulk of the work being conducted between 1900 and 1905 under the direction of the British archaeologist Sir Arthur Evans.

As well as the Neolithic remains, these excavations revealed that there had been many periods of rebuilding before the first palace was founded on the site in around 1900 BC. This building was destroyed by a violent earthquake sometime around 1700 BC, after which the site was extensively rebuilt.

The Minoan golden age

The second palace, the most extensive to have been built on the site, belonged to the golden era of Minoan civilization. At this time, the Minoans were the dominant power in the Agean, trading and establishing diplomatic contacts with ancient Egypt. This period of power lasted until their latter eclipse by the Mycenean civilization of mainland Greece.

The throne room was situated in a series of cult rooms to the west of the central court. The bath in the foreground was for ritual bathing.

How greatly Minoan civilization had by now developed can be judged by the sheer extent and scale of this second palace and its various buildings. Its ruins, arranged around a large paved court, cover an area of 706,289 square feet (20,000 square meters). Approximately 5,000 people are likely to have lived there, with as many as 50,000 living in the dependent territories. For Knossos was more than just a royal residence — it also served as an administrative, religious and economic center, with its king being likely to have held authority over the rulers of the other Cretan palaces.

What we see here is the northern entrance to the palace. The road to the port of Knossos was reached through a gate to the right; the two-storied gallery which can be seen to the left was probably a dining hall. A narrow path led between the two-storied palace buildings to the central courtyard beyond. The life of the palace was centered on this paved court, which was surrounded by various porticoes and galleries. Colorful wall paintings, discovered here and at other Minoan sites, vividly illustrate some of the entertainments that may have taken place, including boxing matches, dance performances and the celebrated bull games, in which young lightly-clad warriors showed off their athletic prowess by somersaulting unarmed over a bull's horns. Such events, in common with many other palace ceremonies, may have had sacred significance, for the ruler of Knossos combined the dual functions of priest with those of king.

West of the central court was a series of what are termed cult rooms. Among these was the throne room, with its majestic gypsum throne, and associated lustral chamber. Other

British ethnographer turned archaeologist Sir Arthur Evans (above) mounted a series of excavations of Knossos between 1898 and 1935, coining the term Minoan to describe the fascinating civilization he had uncovered. This three-dimensional view of the Hall of the Double Axes (right) was realized from his careful sketches and notes.

Evans was first attracted to Crete by the antiquities from the island he saw on sale in Athens and his love affair with it continued all his life. As well as archaeological excavations, he also financed much reconstruction work, for which he has been subsequently criticised.

DISCOVERER OF MINOAN KNOSSOS

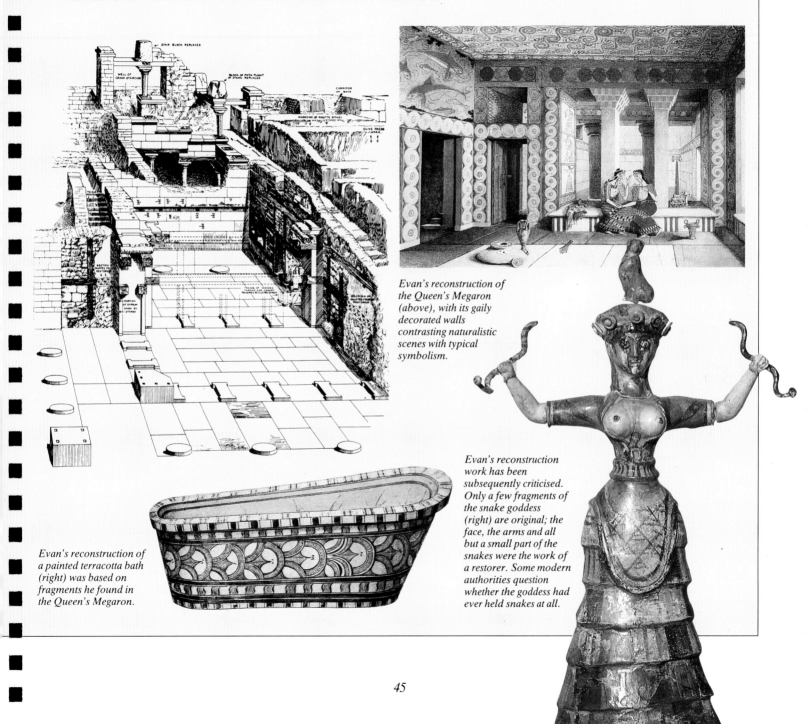

Evan's reconstruction of the Queen's Megaron (above), with its gaily decorated walls contrasting naturalistic scenes with typical symbolism.

Evan's reconstruction of a painted terracotta bath (right) was based on fragments he found in the Queen's Megaron.

Evan's reconstruction work has been subsequently criticised. Only a few fragments of the snake goddess (right) are original; the face, the arms and all but a small part of the snakes were the work of a restorer. Some modern authorities question whether the goddess had ever held snakes at all.

The story of Theseus and his slaying of the bull-headed Minotaur (above), so freeing Athens from the obligation of sending youths and maidens in tribute to Crete, is almost certainly legend.

shrines were scattered throughout the palace. The most significant sacred symbol was the double axe, though its exact meaning remains uncertain. To the east of the court were the brightly painted domestic quarters, set around a series of smaller courtyards.

Storehouses, records and writing

All Minoan palaces were equipped with extensive stores, but those of Knossos were exceptional. Those on the western side of the palace contained as many as 420 huge pottery jars, known as *pythoi*; it is estimated that a staggering total of some 17,150 gallons (78,000 liters) of olive oil could have been stored here. This far exceeded the needs of the royal court, so it is clear that the palace served as a storage and redistribution center.

Obviously, a system of records was necessary if such produce was to be redistributed effectively. Large numbers of burnt clay writing tablets have been found scattered through the buildings, some written in a Minoan script, called Linear A, which, as yet, has not been deciphered, and others in a Mycenean script, known as Linear B and related to actual Greek, which has been translated. This method of regulating and controlling the Minoan economy was facilitated by the geographical location of the various palaces at the centers of fertile agricultural areas, with easy access to coastal ports.

Minoans and Myceneans

Towards the end of the second millenium, Knossos and the Minoan civilization fell into decline. There is no definite reason for this, though there are various theories. What is certain is that the Minoans were gradually eclipsed by the rising powers of mainland Greece – though, again, the reasons for Minoan eclipse have not been firmly established – and that, from about 1450 BC, Knossos itself had fallen under Mycenean domination. Other palaces on Crete seem to have been totally abandoned at this time. Until recently, it was believed that a massive volcanic eruption at the nearby island of Santorini (Thera), which literally blew it apart, had hastened the fall of Minoan culture, as there is evidence of earthquake damage and layers of pumice at many sites. However, recent geological research suggests that the eruption may have occurred some 200 years earlier than was previously believed and cannot therefore have been the crucial factor in the decline.

The date of the final destruction of the palace is equally uncertain; archaeologists have put forward various dates, ranging from 1375 to 1150 BC. However, there is no doubt, for whatever reasons, that the civilization of Bronze Age Greece failed.

The Minoans were great artists; their naturalistic frescoes, painted in vivid colors, provide a fascinating record of palace customs and dress. The bull-leaping fresco (right) apparently celebrates a dangerous ritual, which, as far as we know, was unique to Minoan Crete. In it, young men and women played games with the sacred bull, though no one knows exactly

what this involved. It has been argued, fo. instance, that the somersault depicted here is physically impossible to perform. Another fresco, from the queen's chamber (above), may depict a Minoan queen. She may have been a high priestess, though we do not know for certain where she stood in the Minoan social rankings; however, the elaborate hairstyle and jewelry testify to her importance.

BULLS, FRESCOES AND THE MOTHER-GODDESS

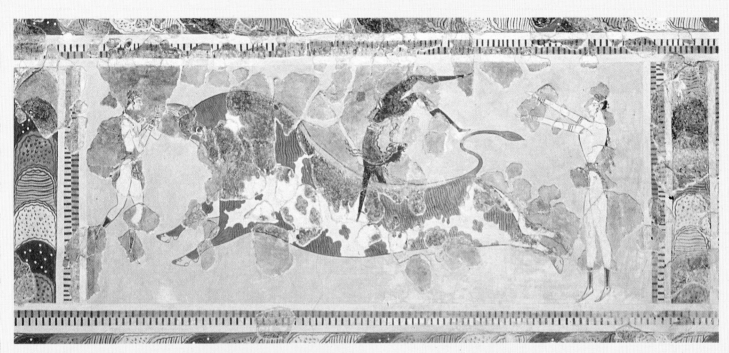

An elaborately decorated fresco, depicting dolphins (left) is a testament to the importance the Minoans placed on the sea and trade. In Greek legend, Minos is described as "ruler of the sea."

The Minoans observed nature closely, as this bird fresco (right) reveals.

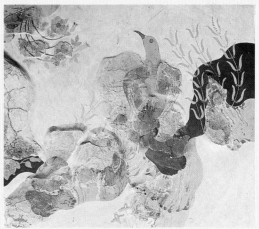

THE ACROPOLIS

*High above ancient Athens, a complex of buildings was erected
that makes up one of the greatest architectural wonders of all time*

Pericles, above, one of the greatest of Athens's statesmen, was responsible for the rebuilding of the Acropolis after its sack by the Persians. He raised the funds by plundering the resources of the Delian League, an alliance of Greek city-states originally formed to co-ordinate defense against Persia.

The Acropolis viewed from the air (right). As a result of Pericles's ambitious efforts, its notable buildings included the Parthenon, the Erechtheum to the north, and the temple of Nike Athena (Athena Victorious). Other features were the Propylaia, the monumental entrance way, and a huge bronze statue of Athena alongside the Sacred Way. The reconstruction (far right) shows the Parthenon viewed through the Propylaia.

Just as it was in the past, Athens today is still dominated by the Acropolis, the 260-foot-high (80 meters) rocky hill whose name literally means "high point of the city." The earliest settlements here date back to pre-historic times, perhaps from as early as 6000BC. Subsequently it was the site of a small Mycenean fortified city and palace. This, the city of Theseus, flourished in the 13th century BC. In the so-called archaic period, from 700BC to 480BC, it was given over exclusively to temples and sanctuaries, although its easily defensible position and fresh water supply — wells had been cut deep into the rock to tap the fresh water springs — meant that it was still a natural place of refuge in time of trouble.

Rising from the ashes

Such was the case in 480BC, when Athens faced assault by the might of the Persian Empire. Despite stout Athenian resistance, the Persians took both city and Acropolis,

An Athenian coin carries the owl of Athena, the city's patron goddess. The Athenians chose her over her uncle, Poseidon, after the two had contended for this honor.

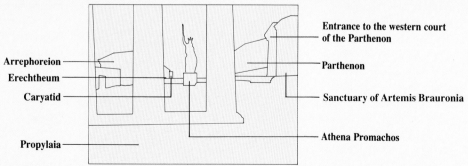

Arrephoreion

Erechtheum

Caryatid

Propylaia

Entrance to the western court
of the Parthenon

Parthenon

Sanctuary of Artemis Brauronia

Athena Promachos

THE ELGIN MARBLES

British peer Lord Elgin (above) removed a major section of the sculptures of the Panathenaic frieze from the Parthenon in 1806 and brought them back to Britain. Their ownership is now a matter of considerable controversy. The frieze, a part of which is shown (right), depicts the Panathenaic procession held to celebrate the birthday of the goddess Athena and may well have been created in the workshop of the great sculptor Pheidias. Women, too, had a role in the celebrations, as the detail from the vase (above right) demonstrates.

The glories of the Parthenon

The Parthenon is probably the most celebrated building of the entire Classical world. Dedicated to Athena, it was created between 447BC and 432BC and was built entirely of the purest marble. Only the doors, doorways and ceilings were timber. The sculptor Pheidias, a close friend of Pericles, supervised the project, Kallicrates and Iktinos being the actual architects. Pheidias sculpted the gold and ivory statue of Athena Parthenos housed inside the temple, dedicated around 438BC and unfortunately destroyed in antiquity — as he did the giant bronze statue of Athena Promachos referred to above and visible in the center of the reconstruction. This depicted the goddess in her role as defender of the city and was so tall that it could be clearly seen from Cape Sounion by sailors on their way to Piraeus, Athens's port. To one side were the covered porticos of the precinct of Artemis Brauronia. Here, Athenian women dedicated colored woolens, silk clothes and articles of toiletry to the goddess.

The chief glory of the Parthenon was undoubtedly its sculptures and statues. In addition to the Athena Parthenos, groups of sculptures ornamented the pediments at each end of the building — the ones at the eastern end depicting the birth of Athena and the ones at the western end showing the contest between Athena and Poseidon as a result of which the Athenians had chosen the goddess as their city's patron. A continuous band of sculpture around the upper part of the walls of the cella, the outer chamber, and the friezes above the porticoes celebrated the Panathenaic Festival. Of the 525 feet (160 meters) of this sculpted frieze, 335 feet (102 meters] are still in existence. The western part is still in place in the Parthenon, but most of the remainder was

razing the latter to the ground. Even the sacred olive tree, which it was believed the goddess Athena had given to the city, was burned, though, greatly to the Athenians' relief, it subsequently put out new shoots.

This could well be taken as a symbol of subsequent Athenian resurgence. The following year, the Persians were finally driven out of Greece and there followed what became recognized as the golden age of Classical Athens. This era was dominated by Pericles, one of the greatest of all Athenian statesmen, and it was under his guidance that the Acropolis was rebuilt. The view here shows the summit of the Parthenon through the Propylaia, the monumental entrance way designed by Mnesicles.

removed in 1806 by the British collector and antiquarian Lord Elgin. These, the celebrated Elgin Marbles, are now in the British Museum.

The Panathenaic Festival

This festival, the most important of all the religious ceremonies of Athens, is linked to the story of one of the other buildings on the Acropolis — the Erechtheum. According to legend, this occupied the site where Poseidon, the god of the sea, had competed with Athena for the right to protect Attica, the region of Greece that contained Athens. The legend tells how the god had struck the ground with his trident, causing sea water to spring forth and offering the Athenians the domination of the seas. Athena, however, won the contest with her gift of an olive tree — and it was this tree, so the Athenians believed, which had miraculously resprouted after Persian sack.

The post-Classical Acropolis

In the Hellenistic and Roman periods, the Acropolis remained the religious center of a city that retained an important cultural role, even though its political significance had waned. In the 3rd century AD, it was once again used as a fortified citadel. Later, under Byzantine influence, the temples were converted into churches.

In 1458, however, the Ottoman Turks captured the city. The Erechtheum became a harem and the Parthenon a mosque. In 1687, when the Venetians attacked the Turkish garrison, the latter used the Parthenon as a powder store, which exploded during the battle, destroying the entire central portion of the building. More damage was done during the Greek War of Independence in 1827, but, following this, intensive archaeological study and restoration work commenced.

TEMPLES, COLUMNS AND ORDERS

The Acropolis is a masterpiece of Greek architecture, as the Porch of the Caryatids, on the north side of the Erectheum shows (above). Greek Classical architects devised a series of guidelines and rules, notably for form and proportion, which continue to influence architectural design even today. One of the key principles they established concerned the design of columns, which fell into three main orders — Doric, Ionic and Corinthian.

Doric capitals (top right) had circular bowel-shaped bases and square tops. In the Ionic order (right), the fluting *of the columns was more pronounced, with the capitals terminating in opposing fluted spirals.*

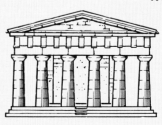

A comparison between the Temple of Poseidon Paestum (far left) and the Parthenon (left) shows how overall architectural style became more refined. Note the common feature – the even number of columns.

THE AGORA

*The meeting place for ancient Athenians, where the idea of
Greek democracy was born*

This vividly-sculpted figure of an Athenian boy was carved to celebrate his victory in one of the running races that featured heavily in the city's games and also in the annual Panathenaic Festival. He is still holding his victory ribbon.

Unlike most other great sites of the Classical world, the Agora, the civic center of ancient Athens where the Athenican experiment with democracy was born, was lost and forgotten until modern times. The mystery of its disappearance was solved only as late as 1931, when archaeologists from the American School of Classical Studies started to find traces of buildings on the site, which they recognized as those described by long-dead historians and writers. The excavations continued and now much of the site has been cleared. The Agora is shown here as it would have appeared towards the end of the 5th century BC, following the rebuilding, first under Kimon and then under Pericles, that followed the sack of Athens in 480 BC and the subsequent Athenian victory at Plataiai during the war with the Persian Empire.

Birthplace of democracy

The Agora itself was simply a sacred area, its boundaries being marked by stones inscribed "I am the boundary of the Agora." Those deemed unfit to enter — according to some definitions, such persons included deserters, those who mistreated their parents and people with dirty hands (for which there was no excuse, since basins of holy water were set at the Agora's entrances for the purpose of washing) — were effectively excluded from public life. The center was crossed by the Panathenaic Way, which made it a key point in the so-called Panathenaic Festivals. Festivals, plays

and games had also been held in the part of the Agora known as the orchestra until the beginning of the 5th century BC, when most had been transferred elsewhere. However, victors continued to be commemorated by monuments erected there.

Athens's principal civic buildings were set below the Hephaisteon, a temple dedicated to Hephaistos and Athena, which dominated the Agora from an adjacent hill. The new Bouleuterion housed the daily meetings of the 500-strong *Boule* (Senate), the principal legislative body. A 50-member executive council, drawn from the *Boule*, met in the adjacent Tholos.

Periods of executive service lasted for 35 or 36 days at a time, during which the selected senators were maintained at the public expense, taking their meals in the Tholos. Normally, Athenians ate reclining on couches, but, in this instance, the senators sat on benches, since the building was simply too small to take the necessary number of couches. Meals were simple, including cheese, olives, leeks, barley, bread and wine – meat and fish did not feature on the menu until the end of the 5th century. The building was constantly manned, a third of the council remaining there on night duty.

Mother of the gods

The old Bouleuterion was converted into a state archive. Though nothing remains of the documents that would undoubtedly have been stored there, several laws were also copied on to stone tab-

The reconstruction (right) shows the Agora as it would have appeared to an Athenian in the late 5th century, looking down on the site from the Acropolis. Note the clearly delineated Panathenaic Way. Many of the buildings here were rebuilt by Kimon and, later, by Pericles, following Athens's sack by the Persians in 480BC.

Coin blanks from the Athenian mint. The coins the mint forged would have been used to pay the storekeepers of the Agora.

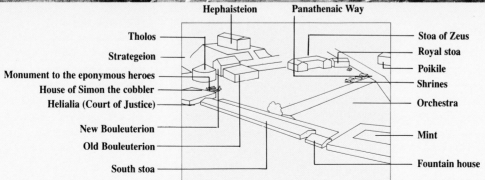

Hephaisteion
Panathenaic Way
Tholos
Strategeion
Monument to the eponymous heroes
House of Simon the cobbler
Helialia (Court of Justice)
New Bouleuterion
Old Bouleuterion
South stoa
Stoa of Zeus
Royal stoa
Poikile
Shrines
Orchestra
Mint
Fountain house

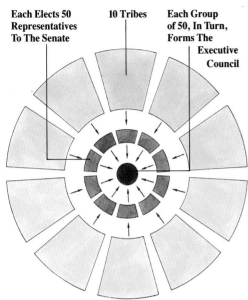

Each Elects 50 Representatives To The Senate

10 Tribes

Each Group of 50, In Turn, Forms The Executive Council

This diagram shows how Athenian government operates at the popular level. Each of the city's districts sent 50 representatives to the Boule (Senate). From these, a 50-strong executive council was drawn, membership rotating between the district groups. Each of these held office for 35 or 36 days at a time.

lets for public display and consequently have survived. This building also came to house the cult of Rhea, the mother of the Olympian gods. Consequently, it was rechristened the Metroon.

Favored meeting place

Two open-fronted stoas were set nearby. The stoa of Zeus Eleutherios was a favored meeting place for Athens's citizens; ancient texts tell us that the philosopher Socrates, for instance, used to meet his students and friends there. The adjacent royal stoa was the seat of an official known as the king archon. Once highly powerful, the office had become largely ceremonial with the advent of democracy, but retained important responsibilities in the field of religious law. When Socrates was accused of impiety and of corrupting Athenian youth, for instance, the case was taken before the archon and it was he who determined that the matter should go forward to trial. In front of this stoa stood the oath stone, one of the oldest features of the Agora. Here, incoming magistrates swore their oaths of allegiance before taking office.

Agora and Poikile

The Agora, too, was the place where all the citizens of Athens — not just the senators — could put democratic principles into practice. During the 5th century, the Athenians took extreme steps to protect themselves against the threat of tyranny. Once a year, the citizens assembled in the Agora to decide by vote if anyone was becoming too powerful. If the answer was in the affirmative, a second assembly was held two months later, at which the citizens voted with *ostraka* (sherds of pottery) on which they had scratched the name of the · candidates they considered deserved ostracism. Whoever received the most votes, provided a minimum of 6,000 had been cast, was exiled from Athens for 10 years.

This system seems sound in theory, but, as archaeological research has revealed, it could be abused in practice. Over 1000 discarded *ostraka* have been found on the site. One group of 190 all bear the name of the Athenian statesman Themistocles, but close examination of the writing reveals that only 14 people had written on them. It would seem that an organized faction of Themistocles's opponents had produced ready-made *ostraka* to distribute to illiterate and undecided voters.

On the north side of the Agora stood the Poikile, which was celebrated for its paintings

The Agora and its various stoa — the modern reconstructions (below and right) are of the stoa of Attalos — were the places where Athenian citizens met to talk, shop, read public notices and debate the minor and the major issues of the day. Here were situated the city's most important civic buildings, including the Bouleuterian, where the senate met in

daily session and the neighboring Tholos, the home of the governing executive council. Membership of the council rotated away the 50-strong groups of senators each of the city's 50 districts elected for service; this was a safeguard to ensure no one group — or individual — could monopolize power.

Here, too, on the Agora itself, the citizens met to decide by vote if any of their leaders was becoming too powerful or tyrannical. An offender was given two months to mend his ways; if he failed to do so, a second assembly could decide to exile him from the city for ten years.

WHERE ATHENIANS MET –
AND WHERE DEMOCRACY WAS BORN

Bone eyelets, from the site of the store owned by Simon the cobbler, near the Tholos.

Iron hobnails (left), from Simon's store. His footwear was obviously popular – Socrates and Pericles were both among his customers.

The base of a cup (left), inscribed with Simon's name. He lived towards the end of the 5th century BC.

Classical footwear (right) had to be hard-wearing. Travel by any other means of transport was a considerable luxury, in which only the rich or the notable could afford to indulge.

This wall-painting of the Athenian philosopher Socrates (right) comes from Ephesus. Socrates spent much of his time teaching and debating on and around the Agora, but his attacks on religious orthodoxy, the abuse of power, and parental and governmental authority made him many enemies. Eventually, he was found guilty of corrupting the morals of the young and condemned to death. The sentence was self-administered — he drank a lethal infusion of hemlock.

and so widely known as the Painted stoa. Here were hung paintings of the Trojan, Amazonian, Spartan and Persian wars. Here, also, hung the shields taken from the Spartans captured in the Athenian victory at Sphakteria in 425/4 BC. These trophies remained on public display for over 600 years and were still on show when the historian Pausanius visited the Poikile in the 2nd century AD. A single shield survived still longer, to be found in the modern archaeological excavations.

Unlike the other stoas, however, the Poikile had no specific function. It was open to all to meet, talk and walk in its shelter. Among the crowd here were beggars, fishmongers, sword-swallowers, jugglers and other street performers; here, too, could be found philosophers in search of an audience. The philosopher Zeno, for instance, debated here and his followers, taking their name from their meeting place, became known as the Stoics. Their influence spread across the Classical world and lasted into Roman times, several of the emperors being influenced by the tenets of the philosophy.

Citizens were also drawn to the Agora to read the notices fixed to the monument of the Eponymous Heroes. This, the city's public noticeboard, was really a form of popular newspaper. There were many stores and workshops around the site as well, which were also popular as meeting places. Socrates, for example, was in the habit of seeing pupils too young to enter the public buildings at the store of the cobbler Simon. This store, also frequented by Pericles, was just outside the square, near the Tholos (excavations here have uncovered a plate marked "Simon" and a large number of hobnails). Some of the most important workshops, concentrated along the road to the Dyplon gate, specialized in the production of Athens's celebrated red-and-black pottery.

The Agora vanishes

The Agora declined in importance in the Hellenistic period, from 323BC to 146BC, although several new buildings were erected there under both the Macedonians and the Romans. The site was finally abandoned after the fall of the Roman Empire.

It was not deliberate policy, however, that led to the Agora's disappearance — or an act of vandalism, war or conquest. The medieval growth of Athens saw houses and streets crowd over the area, the ancient significance of which had long been simply forgotten. It was not until the 20th century that the process of rediscovery began, which has led to the recreation of the Agora as we see it today.

CRAFTS AND TREASURES FROM THE AGORA

Athenian craftsmen possessed substantial skills, as these finds of stunning gold jewelry from excavations on the Agora fully demonstrate. The ring (upper right) is a Mycenean signet ring, decorated with a bull-headed man leading two female captives. The earrings (left), with filigree and granular decoration and pomemgrante pendants, comes from the so-called geometric period; the two earrings (right), though not a set, both depict Eros. They were found at the well at the crossroads in the northwest corner of the Agora.

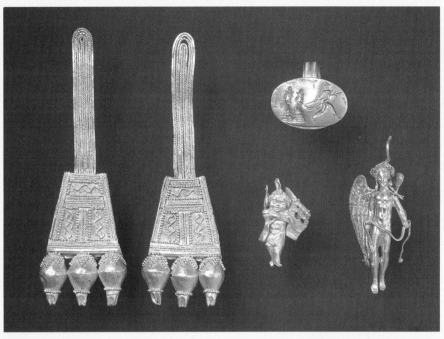

Workshops along the road to the Dyplos Gate were devoted to the production of Athens's famous red-and-black pottery. The red figure vase (left) shows the creation of Pandora. The figures, from left to right, are Zeus, Hermes, Hepheastus and Pandora herself, with Eros above Pandora's head. The Attic red figure cup (right) was decorated by the so-called Meidras Painter, with a wedding scene on its exterior and Aphrodite, the goddess of love, and Pestho on the inside.

THE FORUM

The bustling heart of an empire that stretched across the Classical world

This cramped and cluttered area in the center of Rome, bursting with monuments celebrating a thousand-year history of empire, was itself the setting for many great moments in the city's fascinating history. Its heart, the western end, is shown here as it would have appeared in the 4th century AD. By this time, the Forum had lost any real function, but it remained a rich, complex symbol of Roman imperial power — a place where tourists could gape at the grandeur that was Rome.

Temple of Castor and Pollux
Temple of Saturn
Temple of Vesta
Colosseum
Basilica of Maxentius
Temple of Antonius and Faustina
Arch of Titus
Honorary columns
Basilica Julia
Palatine Hill

Gold coins (above) from the times of two Roman emperors — the bearded Hadrian and Septimius Severus. The Temple of Saturn, at the western end of the Forum, also housed the public treasury, while the Temple of Juno Moneta was the home of an important mint.

The Forum, seen from the Capitoline Hill (left). The original Forum was sited on former marshland, which, according to Roman historians, was drained in the time of Tarquin I, one of Rome's early kings. Several emperors made their own additions, creating a complex that was a magnificent example of civic architecture.

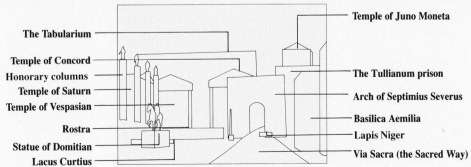

The Tabularium

Temple of Concord

Honorary columns

Temple of Saturn

Temple of Vespasian

Rostra

Statue of Domitian

Lacus Curtius

Temple of Juno Moneta

The Tullianum prison

Arch of Septimius Severus

Basilica Aemilia

Lapis Niger

Via Sacra (the Sacred Way)

A thousand years earlier, this had been an open marshy valley, crossed by the Sacred Way. This led from the original citadel of Rome on the Palatine Hill to the early religious precincts on the Arx Hill. Here the temple of Juno Moneta, the home of the imperial mint, stood, as shown in the reconstruction. The small shrines and cemeteries that were established alongside this road formed the nucleus of the later Forum.

Two early survivals

Two somewhat strange features survived from this early period. One was a small pond, the pond of Curtius, which was an anachronistic relic of the original marsh. Roman religious beliefs undoubtedly lay behind this survival. For the Romans, marshes were mysterious places where the worlds of the living and the dead met, and so were worthy of considerable religious respect. It was here, too, in AD69, a few months after his reign had begun, that the Emperor Galba was assassinated by followers of his rival, Otho, the crowds scattering to safe vantage points to watch the spectacle as the assassins rode into the Forum.

According to Roman legend, the black stone that lay nearby was the tomb of one of the earliest kings of Rome – perhaps even that of Romulus himself. Even today, this stone remains something of an archaeological mystery. Excavations have uncovered no trace of any burial, but an inscription in archaic Latin found beneath the stone dates from no later than the 6th century BC. It refers to regal sacrifice.

The city's center

The area's sacred and historical significance combined with its geographical location at the heart of the expanding city to make it a suitable place for public assembly. Thus, the Forum soon became the center of Rome's political life. Rather like the Athenian Agora (see p43) it served as a busy civic center, with shops and markets dotted around its edges. From the time of the republic onward, it was thronged with crowds, enjoying and contributing to the political dramas of the day. For above all, the Forum was a place for speeches. The Romans made an art of oratory, and listening to the speech-makers was just as much an entertainment as a civic duty.

To one side of the square was the Senate house. On the other were the law courts of the Basilica Julia, the building of which was begun by Julius Caesar to replace an earlier basilica and finally completed in 12BC long after Caesar's death. Caesar's basilica was damaged by fire soon afterward and was comprehensively rebuilt by Augustus, work on it being completed by AD12.

Civil law cases were heard here in front of large and often partisan audiences — some speakers even employed professional cheerleaders to support them when they presented a case. In theory, there was a time limit, measured by water clocks, on how long speeches could last, but dispensations were often granted. Pliny the Younger — Caius Plinius Caecilius Secundus, a noted orator and statesman of the late 1st century AD – was allowed to speak for over five hours, for instance. The Basilica, too, was the scene of a celebrated incident early in the Emperor Caligula's reign, when he climbed onto its roof and stood scattering gold and silver to the people of Rome. According to later reports, some 32 men, 247 women and an eunuch died in the mad scramble that ensued.

The principal setting for public speeches was the Rostra, a stone-built platform reached by a flight of steps. It was decorated with bronze

Designed by Apollodorus of Damascus, the Emperor Trajan's market, a massive five-story brick edifice (above and far right), was a spectacular addition to ancient Rome. The building housed up to 150 individual *tabernae* (booths). Fruit and flowers were probably on sale in the shallow rooms on ground level; at the front of the first floor was a logeria of vast arcades, whose vaulted halls were storehouses for olive oil and wine. Higher still, on the second and third floors, rarer products could be purchased, notably peppers and spices from the mysterious East. The fourth floor housed a hall where *congiaria* (gifts of money or food) were distributed among the populace. On the top floor were fish ponds, one set of which was linked by channels to an aqueduct, so ensuring a constant supply of fresh water.

A Market Built by a Mighty Emperor

This reconstruction (right) of part of a cutler's portable stall shows the kinds of knives and cutting tools available to Roman craftsmen. The bundles in the centre are replicas.

A Roman cobbler (below) was always busy. He sits on a stool, making leather open-work shoes (bottom, right) which were fastened by laces. The stout soles were secured by hob-nails. The craftsman to the cobbler's right is twisting rope.

Market Hall

Via Biberatica

Julius Caesar (inset) was murdered on the steps of the Senate House (left) on the Ides of March in 44BC. His killers, led by Brutus and Cassius, feared he was about to proclaim himself king and put an end to the republic, following his acceptance of life dictatorship a month earlier. They were supported by some 60 senators.

The Forum also contained legacies from the past. This stele (right) bears the earliest known Latin inscription. Though its meaning is disputed, it is thought by some experts to be part of a decree prohibiting the passage of certain beasts, like cattle, in order to maintain the area's sanctity as a place of sacrifice.

A statue of a Roman magistrate. This term was applied by the Romans to all members of the governing classes, from the consuls downwards. The men who presided over the 14 districts into which the emperor Augustus divided the city were called vico-magisters (district magistrates).

captured from the Latins at the battle of Anzio in 338BC. This victory led to the federation of the Latin territories with those of the city and marked a key stage in Rome's progress of expansion. An adjacent column bore the ramming beaks of ships captured in Rome's first success of Rome's newly formed navy against the Carthaginians at the battle of Mylae

in 260BC. Both of these monuments were altered and repositioned by Julius Caesar; it was from the still unfinished new Rostra that Mark Antony delivered his celebrated funeral oration after Caesar's murder on that ill-fated Ides of March in 44BC.

Here, too, were displayed the lists of those condemned to death by the triumvirate of Mark Antony, Octavian and Lepidus, which came to power after Caesar's assassination. Among the Roman notables who were so proscribed was Cicero, whose eloquent speeches had made him one of the star performers in the republican Forum. After his execution, his severed head and right hand were put on public display here.

Triumphs and temples

A recurrent event in the Forum were the triumphal processions of successful Roman generals, who, on their return from their campaigns, were awarded by a grateful Senate the right to celebrate their success by leading a victory parade through the city. These processions, in which the general and his men were accompanied by the trophies of war — including the captives they had brought back to Rome — passed along the Sacred Way and through the Arch of Septimus Severus, which was built to commemorate the victories that emperor had won against the Parthians in Mesopotamia and Assyria between AD195 and 199. In later years, however, the privilege was restricted to the emperors.

At the western end of the Forum – a backdrop to the monuments that have already been described – was the public records office and a series of temples. Among the latter was the Temple of Saturn, one of the oldest temples in Rome, allegedly built on the site of an altar dedicated by the legendary hero Hercules himself. The Temple also housed the public treasury. When Julius Caesar seized control of Rome in 49BC, he promptly plundered 15,000 gold bars, 30,000 silver ones and 30 million sesterces in coin from the treasury to fund his new regime. Classical temples, with their stout walls and carefully guarded treasures, often doubled as banks. To this day, many banks are still designed in imitation of them.

Put to the torch

Moneylenders could also be found in the Basilica of Aemilia, claimed by Pliny the Younger to be one of the three most beautiful buildings of the ancient world. The green lumps and stains still visible on its floor are a grim reminder of the sack of Rome by Alaric the Visigoth in AD410. When his troops set the Basilica on fire, the piles of coins stored there were fused by the heat to produce this effect.

By this time, the Forum was more a museum than a market. Over the subsequent centuries, the area was progressively abandoned and its buildings fell into disuse, though a few of the city's later rulers looked for a little reflected glory by making their own mark on the square. The last monument of any consequence to be erected was a column set up in honor of the Byzantine emperor Phocas in AD602 to 610, though this was hardly original, since it consisted of fragments from earlier monuments.

Several buildings, including the Senate house, were converted into churches and so escaped ruin. But the process of decline continued. By the time that Charlemagne was crowned Holy Roman Emperor at Rome in AD800, Alcuin of York, could lament:
"Rome, once the head of the world, the world's pride, the city of gold.
Stands now a pitiful ruin, the wreck of its glory of old."

LEGENDS OF THE FORUM

Of the various legends connected with the Forum, the best-known is that of Romulus and Remus (below). As boys, they were saved from drowning in the Tiber by a she-wolf; they later decided to found a city on the spot.

Romulus fell out with Remus about the city's location and, having killed his brother, founded Rome. His seizure of the Sabine women (left) led to war between the Romans and the Sabines, which was only resolved by the intercession of the women themselves.

The Temple of Vesta (below) was sacred to the goddess of the hearth. She was served by the vestal virgins, who, from their selection at the ages of between six and ten, swore to remain chaste for 30 years. They tended the perpetually burning sacred fire.

THE COLOSSEUM

*The largest monument of imperial Rome, whose very name
conjurs up a lost world of pageantry, violence – and glory*

*The Emperor Vespasian
(above) ordered the
building of the
Colosseum (below) to*

*start in AD75,
deliberately siting it in
the grounds of what had
been Nero's palace to
win popular favor. The
building was completed
by Vespasian's son,
Titus, in AD79 and soon
became recognized as a
wonder of the Roman
world.*

As the Roman Empire grew, so did Rome to become the greatest city of the ancient world. By the time of the fall of the republic c. 30BC, Rome's population had already passed the million mark, a fact which added to the problems faced by the city's rulers. Because the stability of the city depended on keeping on goodwill of its people, vast sums were spent on feeding and entertaining the urban masses. The loyalty of the Romans was truly won with "bread and circuses".

Over the centuries, partly in response to this need and partly as an act of benevolence, the city was filled with notable public buildings erected by the emperors themselves and by leading citizens seeking to hold on to or win high office. One of the most striking was the Colosseum, a huge amphitheatre built to house the armed-gladiator battles and animal hunts and fights that aroused immense public interest and excitement.

Funerals and a fire

Gladiator shows had their origins in the games that had been organized at the funerals of leading citizens. Such games had first been held in the main public square, or Forum, and had later moved to Rome's first stone ampitheater, which was built by Statilius Taurus around 30 BC. Shortly after this ampitheater was seriously damaged in a

*Gladiators shown in
action on this floor
mosaic (above). They
were divided according
to physique,
heavyweights fighting in
helmet, arm and leg
guards with sword and
shield. Many gladiators
were condemned
criminals or slaves who
had been captured in
war.*

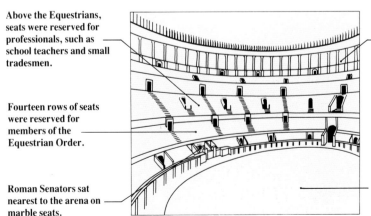

Above the Equestrians,
seats were reserved for
professionals, such as
school teachers and small
tradesmen.

Fourteen rows of seats
were reserved for
members of the
Equestrian Order.

Roman Senators sat
nearest to the arena on
marble seats.

The gallery housed the
ordinary people, seated or
standing. Here, too, a
special area was reserved
for women.

The arena floor consisted
of tight-fitting wooden
planks, over which a layer
of sand was spread.

*The reconstruction
(right) shows the
Colosseum as it would
have appeared shortly
before the Games were
staged. The line drawing
(left) highlights points of
detail.*

WILD BEASTS

Staggering numbers of wild beasts were slaughtered in the Games and new ones were constantly being imported. Many came from Rome's African provinces, lions and elephants being trapped in Libya, while, in the 1st century AD,

Bear against man, a favorite Roman spectacle.

hippopotamus were being transported from Egypt, where they were so common as to be regarded as a pest. By the 4th century, however, the supply of animals from Africa was drying up, so the Romans had to look further afield – chiefly to Persia.

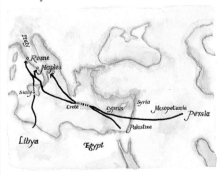

fire, Vespasian, the founder of the new imperial dynasty that came to power after the Emperor Nero's suicide, ordered the construction of the Colosseum to replace the earlier building.

Vespasian chose to build his new creation over the site of an ornamental lake in the grounds of Nero's magnificent urban palace. This, in itself, was a shrewd political move. Nero's response to the great fire that had destroyed vast areas of Rome in AD64 had been to take the opportunity of extending his palace to fill the parts of the city the fire had devastated – a move that the Romans had greatly resented. Vespasian's decision to restore this area to general use was a keen stroke of populist propaganda.

A wonder of ancient Rome

Building started in AD75. It had not been finished by the time of Vespasian's death in AD79 and was completed by his son, Titus, the following year. The result was a marvel of the ancient world – not so much for its design, which was architecturally conservative, but for its size and scale. The completed Colosseum was 190 feet (48.5m) high and 617 feet (188m) by 512 feet (156) across, with seats for between 40,000 and 45,000 spectators and standing room for 5,000 more on its roof.

The sheer size of the audience demanded the devising of a sophisticated ticket system, which, in common with much else in ancient Rome, was based on social class, though admission was free. Numbered tickets directed spectators to the appropriate entrance out of the 76 that were dotted at regular intervals around the perimeter of the building.

Seating by rank

Inside, there were five rising tiers of seats, the best being at the front. The first few rows of

The way in which the Romans brought wild animals into the arena was a triumph of ingenuity, especially considering the basic technology of the day. Two levels of narrow underground passages ran beneath the Colosseum, segmented into eight individual areas, each area being separated from the next. On the lower level, each area contained eight separate cells, into each of which a beast was driven. The cell doors were then shut.

The extensive system of underground passageways running at two levels beneath the Colosseum's arena was extremely complex.

The cells themselves were little more than three-sided cages, which could be physically hoisted up to the second, higher, level. Just before the beasts were scheduled to appear in the arena, their handlers took up position in small rooms at the back of the upper part of each cell and winched the cages up to the higher level. The animals were free to escape – but only along another narrow passageway,

ENGINEERING INGENUITY

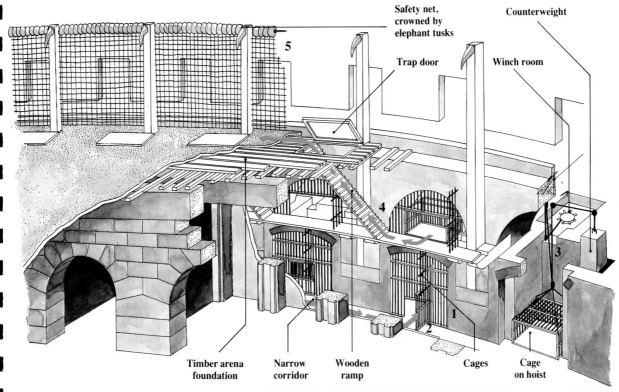

Safety net, crowned by elephant tusks

Counterweight

Trap door

Winch room

5

Timber arena foundation

Narrow corridor

Wooden ramp

Cages

Cage on hoist

4

1

2

3

Wild beasts were brought into the basement area through an entrance at the lower level. They were then herded along narrow passages and into individual cells.

1 *Cell doors and bars. These remained in position when the cages were raised.*

2 *The handlers slammed the open doors shut as soon as the beasts entered the cells. Note how the lower passageway was blocked to prevent the beasts progressing further.*

3 *A rope-and-pulley system was used to haul the cages into position. One end of the rope was attached to a counter-weight; the other runs to a winch in the operator's room.*

4 *Once the cages reached the upper level, the only exit was along a narrow passage, up a ramp and through a trap door into the arena.*

5 *Safety net and ring of elephant tusks protect the spectators, supported by archers.*

corresponding to the one below. Their only recourse was to run up a ramp, through a trap door and so into the arena above.

The timing of the operation was honed to perfection. In a well-staged show, 32 beasts at a time were expected to appear practically simultaneously.

The Roman audience would never have seen the basement vaults, cages and the passages that linked them. The arena floor was boarded over, the boards being covered with layers of sand.

➤ **Animal Route**

PROTECTION FROM THE SUN

The huge canvas awning, or velarium, that protected spectators from the fierce summer sun was hauled into position by teams of sailors from the imperial naval base at nearby Misenum.

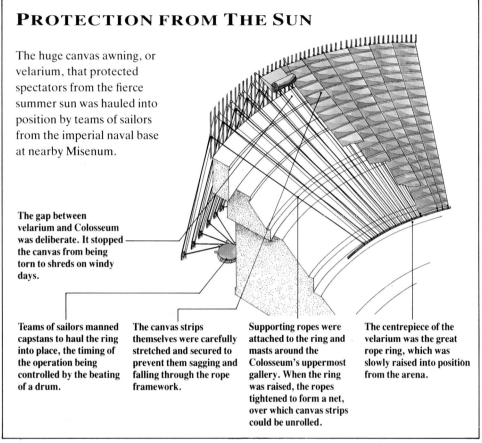

The gap between velarium and Colosseum was deliberate. It stopped the canvas from being torn to shreds on windy days.

Teams of sailors manned capstans to haul the ring into place, the timing of the operation being controlled by the beating of a drum.

The canvas strips themselves were carefully stretched and secured to prevent them sagging and falling through the rope framework.

Supporting ropes were attached to the ring and masts around the Colosseum's uppermost gallery. When the ring was raised, the ropes tightened to form a net, over which canvas strips could be unrolled.

The centrepiece of the velarium was the great rope ring, which was slowly raised into position from the arena.

A canvas awning protected the crowd from the worst of Rome's fierce summer sun.

Fights to the death and animal hunts

The chief entertainments that took place in the Colosseum were gladiator battles and wild animal hunts. These games, as the Romans described them, were held to celebrate a variety of important public festivals and state occasions. The greatest were undoubtedly held to celebrate imperial achievements; the games that commemorated the Emperor Trajan's victories over the barbarians on the Dacian frontier, for instance, lasted a staggering 123 days.

The highlight of most games were the individual contests between pairs of gladiators; in some shows, too, the animals were hunted or baited by men and dogs. Predators could also be set against prey – human victims included. In ancient Rome, Christians really were thrown to the lions.

There were several varieties of gladiator, each being differently armed and dressed. They were based in a building to the east, where their training school was also situated. When it was time for action, they entered the arena via a passage in one of its shorter sides, the bodies of the defeated being carried out through the Porta Libitinaria opposite. The fights themselves continued until death, a serious injury, or submission brought them to an end. In the latter two instances, the loser would plead for his life by raising a finger of his left hand. The response – the celebrated "thumbs up" or "thumbs down" – was given from the imperial box in response to popular reaction.

Gladiators also took part in the lavish animal hunts, which were staged complete with elaborate sets and scenery, depicting, say,

marble, arena-side seats were reserved for Senators, followed by 14 rows for members of the so-called Equestrian Order – the non-aristocratic rich. Then came another sector for citizens of more modest status and, above a circular gallery, the seats for the lower classes. Higher still, at the very top of the amphitheater, an area was reserved exclusively for women. In part, this sex discrimination was intended to discourage promiscuous behaviour in public.

Evidence of this system of division can still be seen today; many of the surviving seats are marked as being reserved "for school teachers," "for public guests" and so on. Each senator had his name chiseled on his seat, the named being removed only on death, or if he was degraded from senatorial rank.

Four entrances to the Colosseum were not numbered. One, on the north side, still preserving traces of elaborate stucco decoration, led directly to the imperial box, which was situated at the edge of the arena. On the opposite side was the entrance to the Consul's box. The other two gates were reserved for other civic and religious dignitaries.

mountains or woods. This was set and shifted extremely efficiently; ramps, hinged platforms and counterweights in the center of the arena were employed to raise or remove complex sets up to 16 feet (5m) high. The system used to cage the animals and bring them to the surface at just the right moment was equally ingenious.

Obviously, with these wild beast shows, spectator safety was an important consideration, especially with leading Roman notables seated at the very front of the audience. For this reason, the arena had a safety net around it. This was capped by a number of downward-pointing elephant tusks, which would have impaled any beast that attempted to jump them. In addition, a band of trained archers was on hand ready to intervene and shoot to kill in any emergency.

Decline and fall

In common with other Roman public buildings, the Colosseum fell into some disrepair in the declining years of the empire. With the coming of Christianity and its adoption by Constantine as the state religion, the gladiator shows gradually came to an end, finally being abolished by Emperor Valentin III in AD438. The animal hunts survived a little longer, the last recorded one taking place in AD523.

Nevertheless, the Colosseum survived to become one of the wonders of present-day Rome and a constant reminder of the glories of the imperial past. As Byron put it in his Childe Harold's Pilgrimage:

"While stands the Coliseum,
Rome shall stand:
When falls the Coliseum, Rome
shall fall:
And when Rome falls – the World."

A DAY IN THE LIFE OF THE COLOSSEUM

AT DAWN: After a banquet the previous evening, the participants and officials set off for the amphitheater, the sponsor of the Games in their midst. He was normally the President of the Games and had to be in constant attendance.

MORNING: In the Colosseum, beasts were hunted or provoked into battling with each other. On an average day, around 100 would be killed. Alternatively, animals performed circus tricks and exotic beasts were paraded.

Towards midday, condemned prisoners were put to the sword, some after public torture.

A fragment of gilded glass (right) shows a retiarius ready for combat, armed with trident and a net, in which he would seek to entangle his opponent.

LUNCH: As it was considered improper for notables to eat and drink in their seats, these left the arena, but the general public snacked on fried chick-peas and nuts, while being entertained by actors and musicians.

AFTERNOONS: Dedicated to armed combat. The gladiators paraded through the arena before the President and their weapons were tested for sharpness. Officials, armed with whips and brands, readied themselves to deter attempted flight. The gladiators then warmed up with mock thrusts and parries.

On the President's signal, trumpets were sounded and the first fight, supervised by two referees, began. The audience was intermittently sprayed with perfumed water to smother the stink of slaughter. Musicians played without a break, pausing only as the death blows were administered.

Hearses, accompanied by an official costumed as Charon, the Etruscan god of the underworld, took the corpses through the Porta Libitinaria (the gate of the goddess of death) and the bravest victor was awarded a laurel wreath and rewarded with gold. At sunset, the Games closed.

Bronze helmets (above) were issued to gladiators armed with shield and sword.

An iron gladiator shortsword (right) was capable of inflicting ugly wounds when skillfully handled.

THE EMPEROR HADRIAN'S VILLA: TIVOLI

Created by one of Rome's greatest and most cultivated emperors, the biggest and most beautiful villa in the Roman world

Hadrian and his wife, Sabina, depicted on the imperial coinage. Their marriage was an unhappy one; when Sabina died rumor spread that she had been poisoned on Hadrian's orders.

In ancient Rome and its empire, anyone who was anybody – from the emperor downward – owned at least one house in the country as well as a town house. The country homes of the Roman ruling classes were usually based on working farms, since, for the imperial aristocracy, farming was still the chief way of generating wealth. It was also a suitably gentlemanly pursuit.

These villas were also retreats, where their owners could escape from the oppressive heat of the Roman summer and the bustle of city life, spending their time lavishly entertaining family, friends and acquaintances. The Emperor Hadrian's villa at Tivoli was excellently suited to all these purposes.

Creating the villa

Hadrian's villa reflects the lighter side of the character of one of Rome's most fascinating rulers. Tivoli was the perfect spot for such an important building project. It lay within easy

This sculpture of Antinous captures all the athletic grace that attracted Hadrian to his young favorite. He, too, died in mysterious circumstances.

A DAY IN THE LIFE OF AN AILING EMPEROR

Hadrian spent most of his later years at Tivoli, plagued with chronic ill-health. This forced him to give up hunting and rich food — his favorite dish was a pheasant, pork and ham pastry.

AT DAWN: Hadrian normally rose at dawn. He washed perfunctorily – his beard saved him the discomfort of shaving — and then readied himself for the main business of the day. This was the morning audience, known as the salutatio.

MORNING: At the salutatio, Hadrian received his courtiers, senators, delegations from Rome and the provinces and foreign ambassadors. Occasionally,

Like many leading Romans, Hadrian frequently wrote on wax tablets with a pointed stylus. The tablets were reusable; the beeswax of which they were made could be melted down and used again.

citizens of lesser rank were also admitted. The audience was a formal affairs, the emperor, dressed in his purple toga, standing to receive his visitors. It was his custom to greet friends with a kiss.

AFTERNOON: After an early, light luncheon, Hadrian usually spent the afternoons relaxing at the baths, walking around the estate, studying or pursuing his various hobbies. The main meal of the day started in the late afternoon, to which philosophers, poets, writers, musicians, mathematicians, orators and astrologers would often be invited to entertain the emperor until it was time for bed.

The *"island villa"* was Hadrian's personal retreat. Here, he could escape from the cares of state and engage in his favorite artistic pursuits without being disturbed. Access to the villa was limited to two small bridges to protect the emperor's privacy.

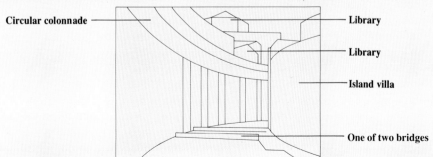

Circular colonnade

Library

Library

Island villa

One of two bridges

reach of Rome on an elevated plateau, swept by cooling breezes and commanding fine views of the surrounding countryside, the city itself being just visible in the distance. Here, there was ample space for Hadrian to realize his lavish architectural ambitions. He himself was something of an artist. He enjoyed painting and, it is alleged, had considerable talent. Above all, he fancied himself as an architect and it is likely that he contributed directly to the villa's design.

The starting point was the original villa on the site, which dated from republican times and may have belonged to the Empress Sabina. Between AD118 and AD138 – the year of Hadrian's death – this villa was extended and eventually a complex of buildings, parks and gardens emerged, which stretched for over half a mile (0.8 kilometers). The complex, as a whole, was larger than some small towns. Within its grounds lay separate guest houses, libraries, baths, temples, a gymnasium, sports stadium and theater, in addition to a series of reception and residential suites designed for use in different seasons.

Some parts of the villa were named after famous places in the ancient world. Others were probably inspired by Greek prototypes, as in the case of the Poikile. This huge courtyard, some 760 feet (231.6 meters) by 318 feet (96.9 meters), was possibly based on the Lyceum in Athens. Such borrowing from Classical Greece would not have been surprising, since Hadrian himself spoke and wrote fluent Greek and had been a devotee of Greek culture since his childhood. This passion earned him the nickname of "the little Greek."

Water and the "island villa"

Water, too, played a major part in the formulation of the overall architectural scheme. In

Hadrian supervised every decorative detail, down to the design of the elaborate floor mosaics that were created for the ospitali and other parts of the villa complex.

addition to its baths, pools and lakes, a large number of ornamental fountains were dotted throughout the complex. To meet the enormous demand that resulted, an aqueduct was specially built to draw water from the River Aniene and carry it to the villa.

The circular "island villa" that is the subject of this reconstruction is a dazzling example of how imaginatively Hadrian used water to help fulfill his plans. This villa-in-miniature was set on a small island enclosed by a circular portico. Its rooms, which included bedrooms, baths and a dining area, were arranged in semicircular groups around colonnaded courts. The result was a striking ensemble of columns and curves, reflections and shade.

After Hadrian's death, the villa continued to be used by succeeding emperors for most of the following century. Some time after that, the complex fell into disuse and ruin. Today, however, its ruins are recognized as a rich source of artistic and archaeological treasures, throwing new light on one of the key periods of Greco-Roman culture.

HOW THE VILLA COMPLEX GREW

Hadrian's villa at Tivoli was the largest and most elaborate ever built in the Roman world. Despite its scale, it was laid out in much the same way as any other Roman villa; what makes Hadrian's achievement unique is the highly innovative architecture of the whole complex, in the planning of which the emperor himself may well have played a key part.

This detail is from the epistyle situated at the north end of the Canopus, a canal-like stretch of water lined with statues, with a temple dedicated to Serapis at its far end.

Water was a central feature in Hadrian's overall plan. The lake here was artificially created to help feed the baths, fountains and pools scattered throughout the complex.

This model shows what the complex must have looked like in its full glory. At its center stood the main villa, which visitors reached via a terrace overlooking the river. From the entrance, they progressed to the formal reception areas, such as the golden square, with its vast audience chamber. On the other side of the villa lay the more private area, with its guest wing, libraries, dining rooms and "island villa". Most of the complex's other buildings were set in the grounds behind the main villa.

Piazza d'oro (reception suite)

Private suite, including libraries

Baths

Academy

Recreational stadium

Canopus

Rocca Bruna tower

Poikile

Island villa

Theater

POMPEII

A volcanic eruption destroys a flourishing city in a few brief hours one sunny summer's afternoon

For the 20,000 or so inhabitants of Pompeii, a prosperous city on the Bay Naples, 24 August AD79 dawned just like any other bright, summer's day. That afternoon, though, the supposedly dormant volcano of Mount Vesuvius above the town exploded in violent and sudden eruption. Millions of tonnes of volcanic debris were thrown up into a vast, lethal cloud and a fall-out of pumice and ash rained down on the surrounding countryside. Pompeii itself was soon submerged beneath 6 feet (1.8 meters) to 12 feet (3.6 meters) of debris. Smaller towns at Herculaneum and Stabiae, together with several villas, were also destroyed, but Pompeii was by far the most devastating loss.

Though the consequences of the eruption were so tragic — thanks to Pliny the Younger we possess a vivid record of the scale of the disaster that so swiftly overtook Pompeii and its inhabitants — for later generations of investigators and archaeologists, it had a beneficial side. The pumice and ash spewed out from Vesuvius actually helped to preserve what the eruption had destroyed, so it was possible to build up a very clear picture of what life in Pompeii must have been like before the disaster.

Bustling streets

Before the eruption, Pompeii had been prosperous and busy. The reconstruction here,

As this street plan shows (below), Roman Pompeii was laid out on a grid pattern and enclosed with stout walls. The via della Fortuna, the subject of the reconstruction (right) is in region six; the oldest part of the city is in region eight. The photograph (left) shows the temple of Apollo (region seven), with a statue of the god in the center and Vesuvius looming in the background.

House of the Mystery

House of the Faun

Temple of Fortuna   House of the Vetii

Bakery

Region V

Region IV

Region VI

Region VII   Region III

Region IX

Region II

Region VIII

Region I

0 50 100   250

Forum

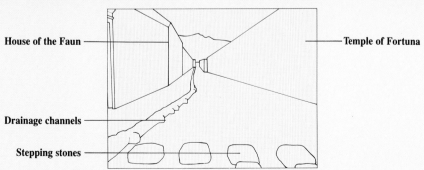

House of the Faun —————————————————————— Temple of Fortuna

Drainage channels ——————

Stepping stones ——————

looking eastward along the via della Fortuna, is a typical street scene. The close-paved road was crossed by stepping stones for use by pedestrians. This was a valuable provision, since many streets would have been little better than open sewers. The street gets its name from the temple of Fortuna Augusta, part of which can be seen on the right. The temple, dedicated to the god-emperor Augustus in 3 BC by Marcus Tullius, a prominent notable, was the first building to be uncovered when systematic archaeological excavation started at Pompeii in 1748. On the left of the street, past a number of smaller homes and distinguished from them by a slightly larger entrance, is the House of the Faun, one of the best preserved Pompeiian houses. Etiquette for entertaining visitors was clear. According to an inscription on the dining-room wall of the aptly christened House of the Moralist, "the slave shall wash and dry the feet of the guests and let him be sure to spread a linen cloth on the cushions of the couches." Behavior for the guests was also clearly defined. "Do not cast lustful glances or make eyes at another man's wife. Do not be coarse in your conversation. Restrain yourself from getting angry, or using offensive language. If you cannot, return to your own house."

In contrast to the apparent comfort of so much of such houses, it is worth noting that some aspects of domestic architecture were extremely primitive. Latrines, for instance, were usually positioned in the kitchen. For all their fabled plumbing, the Romans had little real idea of personal hygiene.

Caught unprepared

The city was caught completely unprepared. Vesuvius had been dormant for many centuries and its slopes were heavily cultivated. Though an earthquake in AD62 had signalled the reawakening of the volcano, the damage this had caused had soon been repaired and life had returned to normal. Beneath the pumice blanket that the eruption left in its wake, there are reminders of the last hours before the disaster. In Modestus's bakery, some bread

Roman townhouses were designed for display – to show off the wealth and sophistication of their owners, such as the Pompeiian lawyer Terentius Neo and his wife (above). In such a house, a narrow corridor led to the atrium (below), the main

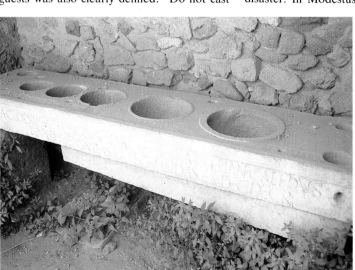

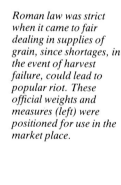

Roman law was strict when it came to fair dealing in supplies of grain, since shortages, in the event of harvest failure, could lead to popular riot. These official weights and measures (left) were positioned for use in the market place.

LIFE IN A POMPEIIAN TOWN HOUSE

Behind the scenes, arrangements were more primitive. It is unlikely, for instance, that guests would have penetrated into the discreetly concealed service quarters, where the household slaves lived and worked. Here were the cramped smoky kitchens, storerooms and latrines.

reception area, which was lit by the light streaming through its partially open roof. Here the head of the household would have conducted an important part of his daily business; it was here that notable men of affairs held their morning receptions, at which their dependants – their clients – would gather to supplicate favors or seek patronage.

Beyond lay the peristyle (above), a cloister-like porticoed garden, which gave access to a further series of more intimate rooms. The most important of these was the triclinum, the

large dining room where supper guests would spend the evening feasting, talking and being entertained, the food and drink being prepared and served by the household slaves, tucked discreetly away in their quarters around the kitchens. Supervising this part of the household was woman's work — in a carefully ordered patriarchal society, Roman men left this sort of thing to their wives.

The photographs here are of the House of the Vettii. Typical of such houses in Pompeii, it was built of solid stone. Similar houses could extend to four or five storeys.

A vibrant wallpainting from the House of the Mystery painted in the 1st century BC. It depicts Silenus and Satyrs showing initiation of brides into the rites of Dionysus.

rolls that had just been put in the oven were left to burn. Elsewhere, the leftovers of lunch were scattered across dining tables.

The bodies of some 2,000 of the victims have also survived, cavities around the skeletons preserving the imprint of long decayed flesh and clothing. The more fortunate ones were killed in the first moments of the eruption by falling debris. Others, perhaps, succumbed quickly to the fumes. Still more were engaged in a protracted battle for survival, as they attempted to flee from the ruins.

The story of a group of priests fleeing from the Temple of Isis is typical. First, they saved what they could from the temple, after which a trail of corpses and abandoned treasure re-veals their fate. One priest quickly collapsed and died at the street corner; others pressed on to the triangular forum, where two were killed by falling columns. The remainder sought shelter in a nearby house, where they became trapped. One of them, desperate to escape from being buried alive to die of suffo-cation, hacked his way through two walls before falling, axe in hand.

Throughout the city, cellars became places of refuge. In one house alone, 34 people re-treated to the basement, well provisioned with bread and fruit and even taking a goat along with them. In the House of the Vestals, a man and a dog were trapped together, the dog sur-viving longer than his luckless master by gnaw-ing at his owner's body. At least one man tried to escape the rising debris by climbing a tree.

The luckiest, though, were those able to make good their escape on horseback. Several carts laden with salvaged goods and belongings were abandoned, the animals which pulled them being unhitched and ridden away.

Famed for its wine

The city so hastily abandoned was already ancient when the eruption struck. Originally, Pompeii had been settled by the Greeks in the 7th century BC, coming under Etruscan and then Samnite control before its capture by Rome at the end of the 4th century BC. The oldest part of the town was the area around

VICTIMS OF THE ERUPTION

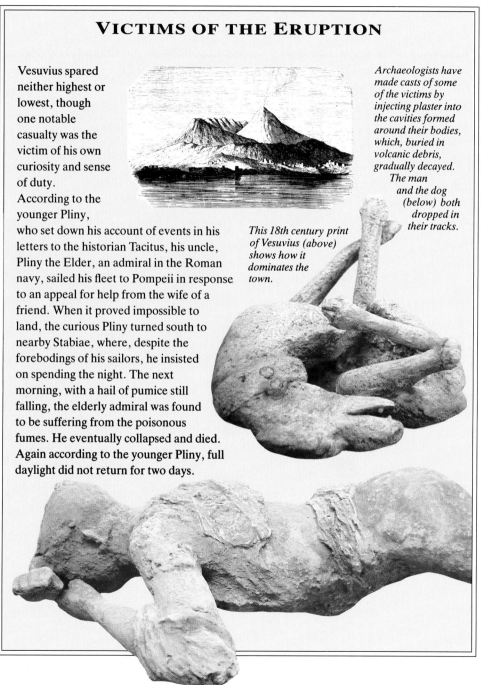

Vesuvius spared neither highest or lowest, though one notable casualty was the victim of his own curiosity and sense of duty.

According to the younger Pliny, who set down his account of events in his letters to the historian Tacitus, his uncle, Pliny the Elder, an admiral in the Roman navy, sailed his fleet to Pompeii in response to an appeal for help from the wife of a friend. When it proved impossible to land, the curious Pliny turned south to nearby Stabiae, where, despite the forebodings of his sailors, he insisted on spending the night. The next morning, with a hail of pumice still falling, the elderly admiral was found to be suffering from the poisonous fumes. He eventually collapsed and died. Again according to the younger Pliny, full daylight did not return for two days.

This 18th century print of Vesuvius (above) shows how it dominates the town.

Archaeologists have made casts of some of the victims by injecting plaster into the cavities formed around their bodies, which, buried in volcanic debris, gradually decayed. The man and the dog (below) both dropped in their tracks.

the Forum, in the south-west corner of the city. Here were most of the principal public buildings — the temples, theaters and council chambers — around which political and social life revolved. Following its conquest by the Romans, Pompeii was enlarged, with a grid of new streets, and enclosed by substantial walls.

Pompeii owed much of its prosperity to its role as an administrative center and market town. In common with the rest of the Roman world, wealth and power derived from land ownership and the chief citizens of Pompeii owned substantial tracts of the surrounding countryside. The area was particularly noted for its wine, although — at least according to the contemporary historian and commentator, Pliny — drinking the local "Pompeiana" could bring on a headache that lasted until noon the following day. Since there were 118 bars and 20 winestores in Pompeii, this claim is likely to have been put to the test fairly frequently. More seriously, the main industries — tanning, baking, fulling and the manufacture of garum, a fermented sauce made from fish entrails — all reflect this dependence on agriculture.

Many tradesmen formed guilds, which became actively involved in promoting the political careers of their patrons and the principal streets were daubed with their electoral slogans. The existence of guilds of dyers, pack carriers, garlic dealers, goldsmiths, fruiterers, wheelwrights, carpenters, plumbers and mule drivers is confirmed through such graffiti.

Abandoned city

After the disaster, the Emperor Titus organized relief programs for the refugees. Some survivors returned to the site to dig for their possessions, but a plan to build a new Pompeii was never realized. The site was simply abandoned, and was only rediscovered in the 18th century.

GLASTONBURY ABBEY

Was this the legendary "Isle of Avalon" to which Joseph of Arimethea bore the Holy Grail and where the heroic Arthur — the "once and future king" — was laid to rest?

Glastonbury's links with legend started in medieval times. Here, according to the chroniclers, Joseph of Arimethea carried the Holy Grail (above); here, too, Arthur was buried. The abbey itself (below) was one of the most important in England.

In the heart of the west of England, Glastonbury Abbey breathes romance, magic and mystery. Here, according to early British histories and legends, lay the isle of Avalon, where St. Joseph of Arimethea, carrying the Holy Grail containing the blood and sweat of Christ, established the first English monastery, his staff taking root on Wearyall Hill to flower as the Glastonbury thorn, which bloomed every Christmas Eve.

Glastonbury, too, is thought to be the resting place of Arthur, the legendary "once and future king," who, so it is believed, will one day rise again to rescue Britain in its hour of utmost peril. It also claims to be the burial place of Guinevere, Arthur's ill-starred queen, who took refuge in a nunnery here after being detected in adultery and fleeing Arthur's court with her lover, Lancelot. Nor

do the legends stop in ancient times. In recent years, some have claimed that the symbols of the Zodiac are hidden in the contours of the surrounding landscape. And there are some who believe that the place is a highly charged and sacred focal point for the generation and transmission of healing cosmic energy.

Legend and truth

Legend, it is clear, breeds legend. As a result, the story of Christian and Arthurian Glastonbury is now so richly elaborated that it is virtually impossible to establish any underlying historical truths. According to a biography written around AD1090, for instance, Glastonbury was founded by St. David, the patron saint of Wales, who died at the end of the 6th century AD. But, early in the 12th century, the medieval historian William of Malmesbury argued that the site had far earlier significance — he was even prepared to countenance the possibility that the abbey there owed its foundation to an apostolic mission. This, no doubt, encouraged the later link with Joseph of Arimethea. Later in the 12th and 13th centuries, the picture was further muddied when, inspired by French romances of the period, Arthur, too, became identified with Glastonbury. The site was also, but

The Chalice Well (above) is fed by the so-called Blood Spring. Legend has it that Joseph hid the Grail here and the waters turned red as a result. The curving fish-like symbol of the Vesica Piscis carved on the well's cover features heavily in much early British church architecture.

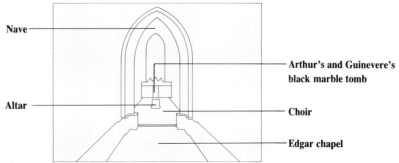

Nave

Altar

Arthur's and Guinevere's
black marble tomb

Choir

Edgar chapel

Some still believe Arthur lies buried under Glastonbury Tor (above). Others hold that the Tor is a focal point for the generation and distribution of healing cosmic energy.

improbably, linked with a mission of St. Patrick from Ireland to convert the pagan Angles and Saxons.

Excavations on the site of the abbey, concentrating on the cemetery that surrounded the early wattle church, have helped to bring some order out of the chaos of myth and legend. They indicate that a monastic settlement was certainly established here in the 6th or 7th centuries, possibly by AD600. This may therefore have been a foundation of the Irish church — even if St. Patrick was not himself involved — and hence one of the earliest monastic sites in England. Remains of an Iron Age lake village have also been found.

However, the graveyard, surrounded by a great bank and ditch and filled with stone-lined graves, post-and-wattle oratories and funerary monuments, had not been left untouched by previous generations. In 1190, the abbey's monks had dug up what they claimed to be the tomb of Arthur, the site of which, according to reports of the discovery, had been revealed to them by miraculous signs and portents. It was set between two magnificently carved house-shaped tombs, alleged to contain the relics of St. Indract, the son of an Irish king who may have been martyred nearby while on a pilgrimage to Rome in the 9th century, and those of St. Patrick himself. At the bottom of the grave, beneath the remains of two or three skeletons, was a small lead cross, which had been inscribed with the short sentence "Here lies Arthur, the famous king, in the island of Avalon."

The cross has been lost, but a 17th-century drawing of it shows the lettering of the inscription to be in the style of the 10th or 11th cen-turies. Nor was any supporting evidence found when part of the grave was rediscovered during archaeological excavations in 1962. The British archaeologist Dr. Raleigh Radford suggests that the cross, therefore, may have been made by a previous generation of monks, who had razed the graveyard and covered over the original tomb in the 10th century.

Centuries of pilgrimage

This would not have been the first time that priests had fabricated relics to win prestige for their monastery and attract pilgrims to it. Glastonbury's pilgrims added to the growing wealth of the abbey, which already ranked as the richest English monastery when the Domesday Book was compiled in the 11th century. The monks lived on the profits and produce of the abbey estates. In addition to their extensive land holdings, the nearby river supplied them with eels and fish. According to a register of 1333–4, the abbey gardener provided the community with garlic, wine from the abbey vineyard, hemp, madder, flax, apples and pears, beans, leeks and onions. William of Malmesbury recorded that the monks were accustomed to eating fish or eggs on several days of the week, while on holy days they were also served with cups of mead, fine wheaten cakes and measures of wine. This taste for good living grew; in later years, the monks sent to London for better-quality fish with which to stock their fish ponds, spices and special wines.

The abbey's ruins, as they exist today, are the remains of an extensive rebuilding program occasioned by a fire, which destroyed the original monastic buildings in 1184. Construction work continued well in to the 14th century, with the vaulting of the nave of the church being completed between 1323 and

THE LEGEND OF THE "ONCE AND FUTURE KING"

Arthur is one of the most romantic and mysterious figures of early British history. Though the majority of the tales about him and his Court of the Round Table date from medieval times — many of them, in fact, originating in France, rather than England — it seems likely that in the period following the Roman withdrawal an Arthur-like figure may well have existed.

Perhaps he was a native Romano-British war-lord who tried to hold at least part of the country together in the face of barbarian attack and invasion.

An effigy of Arthur in medieval armor (left) reflects his growing importance in the romances and histories of the period. He is seen seated at his Round Table, surrounded by his knights (above); the manuscript (below) shows his crowning.

1334. The Edgar Chapel, the subject of the reconstruction here, is later still; it was founded in around 1500 to house the monuments of the early Saxon kings whom the abbey claimed as patrons. Chief among these kings was the 10th-century Saxon ruler Edgar, who had been a great benefactor of the abbey and was buried there. His subsequent disinterment by Abbot Aethelward in the 11th century added another myth to the abbey's rich store of legend. When the king's body was exhumed, it was found to be miraculously preserved; when Aethelward ordered it to be hacked into smaller pieces in order to fit into a new reliquary, the remains began to bleed.

Dissolution and destruction

Shortly after the completion of the Edgar Chapel, under Abbot Richard Whiting, who took office in 1525, the abbey met with a disaster that no miracle could circumvent. In 1536, after his break with Rome, Henry VIII ordered the dissolution of the monasteries. The inoffensive but unfortunate Whiting was arrested and taken to London, where he was imprisoned in the Tower. Later, he was tried on a trumped-up charge of robbery, condemned to death and transported back to Glastonbury for execution in 1539.

Whiting was tied to a hurdle at the abbey gates and then dragged up to Glastonbury Tor, where he was hanged and his body quartered. Within the abbey, the work of destruction had already begun. Its buildings were torn down and its stones used as a source of building material by local notables. The remains that survived did so neglected — until the present century, when renewed interest in the Arthurian legends and an increased awareness of the importance of national heritage once again made Glastonbury a place of pilgrimage.

THE TOWER OF LONDON

*Mighty fortress, royal palace and grim place of
imprisonment and execution beside London's Thames*

The Tower of London, famed in British song, story and legend, is the most celebrated of all English castles. Originally it was one of three fortifications built around the city by William the Conqueror in the wake of his victory over Harold at the battle of Hastings. Their purpose was self-evident — to protect and, at the same time, to dominate and intimidate what, for the Normans, was still an alien capital.

William's fort was built of wood and set in the angle formed by the surviving Roman city wall and the Thames. It was replaced, some time after 1077, by the imposing stone keep now known as the White Tower, which was built by Gundulf, Bishop of Rochester, on royal command. The reconstruction here shows the Tower as it would have appeared some 200 years later in the mid-13th century, after Henry III had rebuilt and greatly enlarged its outworks (a further ring of defenses was later to be added by Henry's son and successor, Edward I). The White Tower, which also contains a chapel dedicated to St. John the Evangelist, remained broadly unchanged during this period of rebuilding, though it was now given the coat of whitewash that inspired its name.

A gold noble decorated with a ship from the time of Henry IV, the reverse of a coin minted to commemorate the marriage of Henry VII and Elizabeth of York, and a testoon (a 12-pence piece) from the same king's reign. The royal mint may have been set up in the Tower as early as 1248; it remained there until 1812, when it was moved to a new building on Little Tower Hill.

Stronghold and palace

Within the Tower's walls, too, lay one of the principal residences of the kings of England, several of whom, from Richard II to Charles II, set off from here for their coronation at Westminster. The royal apart-

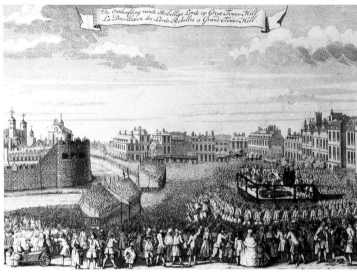

ments were originally located on the first floor of the White Tower and could be reached by an external timber stairway facing the river. Later, in the 13th century, Henry III built a new palace in the area between the White Tower and the river defenses (these buildings were destroyed in the 17th-century English civil war), while in the 1500s, Henry VIII ordered new and more spacious royal apartments to be created in the curtain wall by the river.

It was here that Henry stayed with Anne Boleyn on the night before her coronation on 1 June 1533. As the Tower's function as a royal palace was by now in decline, the king rarely, if ever, returned — but the ill-starred Anne was less fortunate. Following her arrest for

Public executions drew crowds from all over the capital; this Dutch print (above) shows the scene on Tower Hill when four Scottish nobles were put to death in 1746, having been tried for complicity in the unsuccessful Jacobite rebellion of the previous year. At least the axe was quick. Less noble offenders could be hung, drawn and quartered.

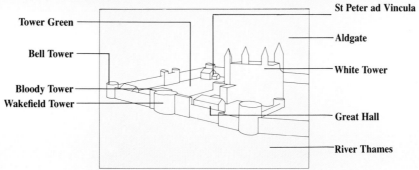

Tower Green
Bell Tower
Bloody Tower
Wakefield Tower
St Peter ad Vincula
Aldgate
White Tower
Great Hall
River Thames

high treason, she was held prisoner in the so-called Bloody Tower (another part of the building), from which she was led to her trial and subsequently to her execution on Tower Green.

A place of grim imprisonment

Anne was not the first — nor the last — notable prisoner to be confined within the Tower's grim walls. Political prisoners were always likely to be incarcerated in a royal castle, where they were directly under the sovereign's control. Initially this had been an occasional and secondary function of the Tower, but over the centuries it became a paramount one, with scarcely a dungeon or chamber empty of prisoners. When the Jews were expelled from England in 1290, hundreds were rounded up

and brought to the Tower before their deportation; similarly, after the battle of Agincourt in 1415, the flower of the French nobility was held captive here until their ransoms were paid. Among their number was Charles, Duke of Orleans, who remained an English prisoner for 25 years.

Life for royal prisoners was not always totally unpleasant, however. They lived in their own comfortable apartments, with chaplains and attendants in tow. Among the most notable royal victims of the Tower was Henry VI, overthrown by Edward, Duke of York (later Edward IV), his rival for the throne. He remained close captive there for five years. Later, the wheel of fortune turned full circle, with the incarceration of Edward's young sons, the Princes Edward and Richard, in the Bloody

Tower, supposedly for their own protection. Aged 12 and 10 respectively, they are known to history as the "princes in the Tower," and the manner of their death still gives rise to speculation. According to tradition, the two boys were murdered or starved to death on the orders of their uncle, Richard, Duke of Gloucester; others argue that Henry Tudor, who eventually defeated Richard (now Richard III) at the battle of Bosworth Field in 1485, was the villain.

Whatever the truth, the Bloody Tower was fast earning a reputation. Originally, up to around 1278, it had been the watergate to the castle, but then a new river gate, now known as the Traitors' Gate, was added. Not only was it easier for kings to reach the Tower by river; it was safest to bring prisoners there by

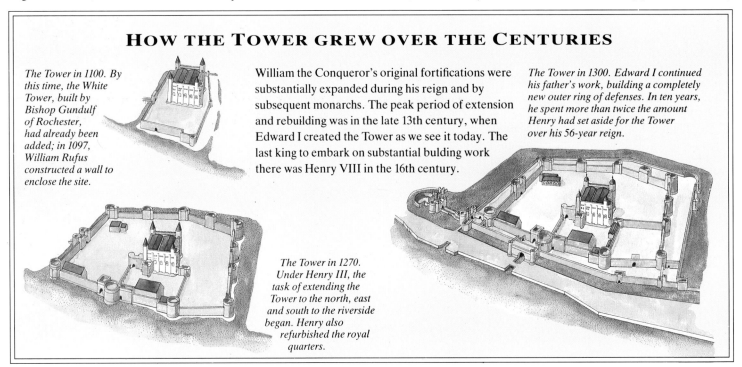

HOW THE TOWER GREW OVER THE CENTURIES

The Tower in 1100. By this time, the White Tower, built by Bishop Gundulf of Rochester, had already been added; in 1097, William Rufus constructed a wall to enclose the site.

William the Conqueror's original fortifications were substantially expanded during his reign and by subsequent monarchs. The peak period of extension and rebuilding was in the late 13th century, when Edward I created the Tower as we see it today. The last king to embark on substantial bulding work there was Henry VIII in the 16th century.

The Tower in 1300. Edward I continued his father's work, building a completely new outer ring of defenses. In ten years, he spent more than twice the amount Henry had set aside for the Tower over his 56-year reign.

The Tower in 1270. Under Henry III, the task of extending the Tower to the north, east and south to the riverside began. Henry also refurbished the royal quarters.

In the basement of the White Tower stood the rack, the main instrument of torture. The other was the so-called Scavenger's Daughter, which compressed its crouching victims as opposed to stretching them. According to the Tower's records, the last person to be put to the rack there was John Archer in 1640. He had been accused of taking part in an attack on the unpopular Archbishop Laud's palace.

The tower menagerie came into existence in 1235, when Henry III was given with three leopards by the Emperor Frederick II.

the same route. The most celebrated prisoner to reach the Tower in such a manner was the young Princess Elizabeth (later Elizabeth I), who was imprisoned there by order of her sister, Mary I.

Another notable prisoner of the Tudor period, Sir Walter Raleigh, had the misfortune to be sent to the Tower twice. His imprisonment was originally ordered in 1592 by Elizabeth I, as a punishment for secretly marrying Elizabeth Throckmorton, one of the queen's Maids of Honor. This period of captivity was to be brief, but, under Elizabeth's successor James I Raleigh was not to be as fortunate. Charged with treason but saved from the executioner's block by a reprieve, he lived in the Bloody Tower from 1603 to 1616 with his wife, son and three servants.

Torture chamber, treasure house and a zoo

Not all prisoners were treated as generously. Although not as extensively employed at the Tower as is sometimes believed, the use of torture reached a peak under the Tudors and Stuarts. Between 1540 and 1640, some 48 warrants authorizing torture were issued, mostly under Elizabeth I. Of these warrants, 11 involved charges of robbery, five of murder, 14 of sedition, nine of treason and nine "religious offenses." In most of them, the rack, invented in 1446 by John Holland, Duke of Exeter and Constable of the Tower, was employed as the instrument of torture.

Executions themselves rarely took place within the Tower, although some of its most notable prisoners, such as Anne Boleyn in 1536 and Lady Jane Grey in 1554, died on the block on Tower Green. Most executions occurred just outside the Tower, on Tower Hill, where 112 people are known to have perished. Several prisoners managed to escape, however. Some swung to freedom from ropes hung from windows; in the 18th century, one — Lord Nithsdale was even able to walk out disguised in his wife's clothes.

The Tower was not just a prison, however. Although it was no longer a royal residence, from the time of the early Tudors onward it retained many of the functions adopted in its earlier years. The Royal Mint, for instance, which had become established in the Tower by the end of the 13th century, was housed there until 1812. The Royal Menagerie, a large collection of exotic animals started by Henry III in 1235 with three leopards given to him by the Emperor Frederick III and a polar bear from Norway, which used to catch fish in the Thames, moved to London Zoo in 1831. The Crown Jewels and royal armories remain.

For the Tower today is still a symbol of the English state and of its governing institutions. Under William the Conqueror, it stood as witness to the brute force he employed to justify his conquests. Today, instead, it manifests the historical tradition and precedent that epitomizes Britain's historic heritage.

MESA VERDE

*Deep in a Colorado canyon, the cliff dwellings of the "ancient people"
still stand as a testament to the diverse talents of the Anasazi*

Look back 800 years ago, to the days when the Anasazi, the "ancient people" prospered over an enormous area of the North American southwest. Their story is fascinating, dating back to the time they emerged as the third, the latest and most extensive group of people to dominate the region in prehistoric times. Their activities were centered on the area where modern Arizona, New Mexico, Utah and Colorado meet and their influence and power was at its greatest between around AD900 and 1100.

At first, the Anasazi settled in small villages near rivers or on uplands, where there was fertile wind-blown soil. They were successful farmers, raising corn, beans and squash; they hunted the local game; they made pottery, as well as a variety of bone, stone and wooden tools. Then, as their communities grew, there came a change. They became cliff-dwellers, living in densely-populated pueblos, concentrations of closely-packed stone-walled rooms that sometimes held as many as 1000 people. This is the story of the pueblos of Mesa Verde and of its fabled Cliff Palace, rediscovered by Richard Wetherill, a Mancos cowboy, as he was pursuing stray cattle in 1881.

Deep in the cliffs

Mesa Verde lies in the north and north-west of the San Juan Basin, an area of high plateaux and deep canyons covered with juniper bushes

The first Anasazi were farmers, living in pit-houses mainly located on top of the mesa. They were also considerable craftsmen, making such tools as axes (inset, left). In the mid-12th century, the move into the canyons began; there, they built their cliff dwellings, including the religious shrines they called kivas (below).

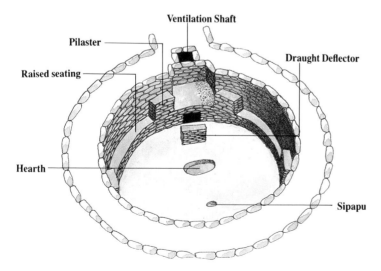

Ventilation Shaft

Pilaster

Raised seating

Hearth

Draught Deflector

Sipapu

Living quarters

Living quarters

Wooden ladder

Kiva

Kiva

and pinon trees. No one knows what drew the Anasazi there and what made them decide to live in its deep, isolated canyons, with most of their fields high above them. Perhaps it was for defense, for their settlements could only be reached down narrow, steep paths. Perhaps it was because the most abundant water supplies were to be found within the canyons. Though the rainfall is somewhat higher in the area than elsewhere in the southwest, it is still irregular and so the Anasazi became expert at conserving the precious water supplies in order to irrigate their maize and bean gardens.

Whatever the reason, the Anasazi were extremely successful farmers in a harsh and demanding environment. Mesa Verde's canyons provided them with many springs and water seeps, plus dozens of natural overhangs in the high cliffs, where pueblos could flourish in perfect isolation. These small farming villages consisting of six to ten pithouses were established as early as AD 600.

Domestic tasks were usually performed outdoors. Specific areas were set aside for such individual activities as weaving, basket-making and corn-grinding (above).

The Cliff Palace

Pueblos were an extremely thermally efficient way of adapting to the extremes of the southwestern climate, with its long, hot summers and bitterly cold winters, as the combination of thick walls and adjacent rooms kept temperatures inside the complex relatively constant. By about 1100, some 2,500 people were living here, most in the Cliff and Fewkes Canyons.

The so-called Cliff Palace was the largest settlement, consisting of 220 rooms and 23 kivas, or "sacred houses", where clan ceremonies took place. Today, if you look down from the canyon edge, you will still see a cluster of the remains of rooms, towers and subterranean chambers huddling under the high cliff overhang. From this, it does not take much

imagination to conjure up what the Cliff Palace must have been like on a late summer's day, 800 years ago.

Anasazi life revolved around the annual round of planting and harvest and was regulated by a rich and complex ceremonial that centered on their *kivas*. Each *kiva* was built to a more-or-less standardised design, consisting of a subterranean chamber with a roof of carefully-shaped beams, thatch and clay, entered through a roof doorway and via a steep wooden ladder. Toward the back of the *kiva* between fireplace and rear wall was a hole in the floor, This, the *sipapu*, was the route from the underworld to the world of the living.

Judging from modern Pueblo Indian society, each *kiva* was owned by an individual clan group. It was here that Anasazi men gathered to organize ceremonies, harvest rituals and initiation rites. It was here, too, that secret societies met and dances took place. The Cliff Palace was therefore both a small town and a ceremonial center, a place where the people of Mesa Verde gathered for important ceremonies and major rituals.

The town flourished for many generations, for as long as the rains were relatively abundant. Then, around 1300, a long cycle of drought settled over the southwest. Though this cycle of drought may not have been as significant a factor in Anasazi fortunes as was previously thought, a decline nevertheless followed. Some archaeologists argue that the reason for this lay in an expanding population, which led to factionalism and so made the Anasazi system of democracy unworkable. The answer was the formation of new, smaller communities. Whatever the reason, another change took place. The pueblos were abandoned and the Anasazi migrated south and southeastward.

THE CRAFTS OF THE ANASAZI

Not for nothing did the first Anasazi become known to archaeologists as the "Basketmakers;" crafts played an important part in their development. Pottery, for instance, was a highly regarded skill, beginning with simple, undecorated pitchers, bowls, jars, dippers, mugs, ladles and canteens and progressing to decoration with a red earthy wash or appealing geometric patterns. Between about AD900 and 1300, the Anasazi potters reached the heights of their skill.

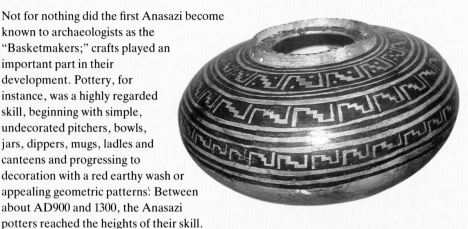

Woven cloth (above). For the Anasazi, such a task was a woman's job, while the men farmed or hunted.

Animal furs and hides had their uses, too. This is woven rabbit's fur (left).

This bowl and ladle (above), jar (top) and drinking mug (far right) are all fine examples of Mesa Verde pottery. Anasazi decorative design was usually abstract, though sometimes stylized birds, animals and human figures appear.

Yucca fiber (below) was used by Anasazi women for weaving.

TEOTIHUACAN

The Pyramid of the Moon towers at one end of a vast complex of palaces and temples — part of the first city to be built in the Americas

Teotihuacan, the first city in the Americas, ranks as one of the most remarkable archaeological sites of the New World. The ruins of this metropolis include 2,600 major structures and are spread over eight square miles (20.7 square kilometers).

The city's heyday was between AD300 and 600. During this time, it covered a greater area than that of contemporary imperial Rome, although with a maximum of between 75,000 and 200,000 inhabitants, its population was less than a fifth of Rome's. The inhabitants held sway over a territory covering the whole of central Mexico and Honduras.

Legends and truths

There are no written histories of Teotihuacan, its builders, or its people. Though it is likely the inhabitants of the city were literate, no

A metate (left) (the traditional corn-grinding stone). In common with other Mesoamericans, the inhabitants of Teotihuacan were skilled farmers. They devised sophisticated irrigation and drainage schemes to improve the yield and quality of their crops.

FRESCOES, MURALS AND WALL-PAINTINGS

Teotihuacan's civilization produced some considerable artists. Almost every wall in the city was decorated with frescoes and murals. Most subjects were religious; some archaeologists believe that they were selected by priests.

An elaborately worked frieze (far left) and a striking red-and-gold mural (left) show the skills of Teotihuacan's artist-craftsmen. The stucco decoration (above) comes from the Temple of the Feathered Shells.

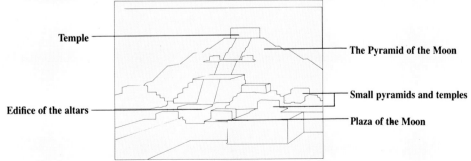

Temple

The Pyramid of the Moon

Edifice of the altars

Small pyramids and temples

Plaza of the Moon

113

writings by them have survived. There are only a few enigmatic symbols, painted on walls or marked on pots. The lack of written records means we do not know what language was spoken, or even what the city and its people were really called. Even the name "Teotihuacan," which means "the home of the gods" or "the place where the gods were conceived," was given to the ruins by the later Aztecs.

Archaeology, however, has revealed that Teotihuacan was built at about the time of the birth of Christ in a small but fertile opening into the northeast side of the valley of Mexico. It has also shown that the city was laid out according to a precise grid, demonstrating that its founders had an impressive mastery of the principles of town planning, and later grew in a series of controlled phases of expansion. What it does not reveal is exactly why the city was founded here, though its creation may well be linked to agricultural practice in the region.

The cultivation of the marshy borders of the Great Lake, which dominated the valley of Mexico, would have required considerable social organization in order to establish the necessary complex irrigation and drainage systems. Engineering work on this scale would have encouraged and reinforced the centralization of power, so providing an important stimulus to the growth of urban centers.

Trade is also likely to have contributed to the success of the city — some Teotihuacan goods have been found as far south as the Guatemala highlands, while Teotihuacan influence has also been detected in the Maya lowlands and the valley of Oaxaca. This is confirmed by evidence from the Aztec period, by which time a special caste of armed merchants, called *pochteca*, had emerged, traveling widely in search of exotic goods and products destined for the king. Representations

of the god they worshipped have been found at Teotihuacan, which suggests that the caste had its origins there.

Pyramids of Moon and Sun

The city was laid out around a broad central way, more than two miles (3.2 kilometers) long and 50 yards (45.7 meters) wide. This was known to the Aztecs as the Avenue of the Dead. The main religious centers were situated on either side of the avenue.

At the northern end of the avenue stood the plaza of the Pyramid of the Moon, the subject of this reconstruction. The massive main pyramid dominated the square, with small pyramids topped by temples surrounding it. In front of the pyramid was an unusual rectangular enclosure, containing a group of ten altars. These, in conjunction with a platform near the center of the square, would have been used in the performance of the religious rites practiced by Teotihuacan's inhabitants.

Farther down the Avenue of the Dead was the Pyramid of the Sun. This imposing edifice, 216 feet (65 meters) high and covering about ten acres (four hectares) at its base, is the tallest pyramid in the whole of Mesoamerica. At the southern end was an enclosure of palaces and temples — the Citadel — which may have been the administrative center of the city. At the enclosure's heart was a temple dedicated to Quetzalcoatl, the feathered serpent god easily recognized as the central figure in the sculptures carved on the exterior.

Priests, nobles and citizens

Teotihuacan was not simply a religious center. It was a fully fledged city, with a large population engaged in a variety of activities. Undoubtedly, though, it was dominated by its priests and nobles, whose houses were clus-

ALONG

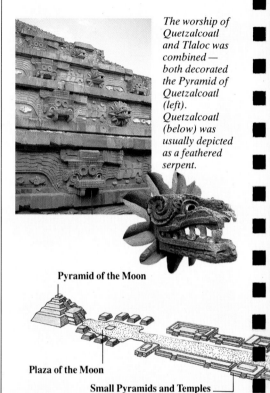

The worship of Quetzalcoatl and Tlaloc was combined — both decorated the Pyramid of Quetzalcoatl (left). Quetzalcoatl (below) was usually depicted as a feathered serpent.

Pyramid of the Moon

Plaza of the Moon

Small Pyramids and Temples

THE AVENUE OF THE DEAD

The Avenue of the Dead (below) led from the Citadel to the Pyramid of the Moon. Notable landmarks along the route included the Plaza and Pyramid of the Sun, the Jaguar Palace (bottom left) and the Quetzalpapalotl Palace. Other features included another plaza complex, a group of four smaller temples, sculptures of mythical animals and the Plaza of the Moon.

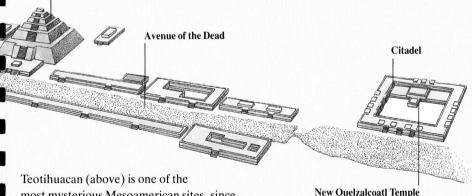

Pyramid of the Sun

Avenue of the Dead

Citadel

New Quelzalcoatl Temple

Teotihuacan (above) is one of the most mysterious Mesoamerican sites, since no writings have survived from its original culture. The later Aztecs believed that the city had been built by a race of giants on the site of the birthplace of the Fifth Sun, after the four previous creations of the world had ended in darkness and destruction. For the city's first inhabitants, however, the most important gods were Tlaloc, the god of rain, and Quetzalcoatl, the bringer of civilization. Lesser deities included a goddess of water and a god of death.

tered around the religious centers. Many of these houses were exceptionally large; some palaces contained more than 75 rooms, built around a series of corridors and inner courts.

It seems likely that several of the street blocks were occupied by a single clan, with the rooms housing individual families opening onto large inner courtyards, in which a temple was located. This inner courtyard was the sole source of natural light, as the outer walls were left blank and windowless. Some city districts, too, were set aside for specialist crafts and trades. More than 500 workshops have so far been identified, including those of potters, stonemasons, bricklayers and plasterers. The majority, however, were obsidian workshops. Objects worked in this volcanic glass were traded extensively and the trade was an important factor in the urban economy. Concentrations of imported pottery in some parts of the city could imply that some districts were occupied by immigrant communities.

Fall of Teotihuacan

Teotihuacan flourished until around AD750, when the latest buildings were burnt and abandoned. Though archaeologists have suggested that the city had fallen to a popular uprising or an invading force, it seems unlikely that either factor, alone or in combination, could have brought about the destruction of this mighty city and its civilization. There must have been some other fundamental cause, but exactly what this was is still unknown.

What we do know, from other Mesoamerican examples, is that such a fall was not unique. The other great civilizations of the area were also to fail in the following centuries and, by AD900, a Mesoamerican dark age had set in, which lasted until the rise of the Aztecs around 1325.

MACHU PICCHU

Deep in a wild, inaccessible Peruvian valley stands the best-preserved and most mysterious of the lost cities of the Incas

A panoramic view (right) of fabled Machu Picchu from one of its watch-towers. Abandoned in the face of the Spanish conquistadores *in the 16th century, the city stands above the canyon of the Urubamba, the sacred Vilcanota of the Incas, and between two Andean mountains. These are Machu Picchu, after which the ruins were named, and its neighbor, the massive Huayana Picchu.*

Deep in the wild, inaccessible Urubamba valley in Peru lies Machu Picchu, the fabled lost city of the Incas. Its remains lay buried and forgotten for centuries, until their rediscovery by Hiram Bingham, an archaeologist from Yale University, in 1911. This rediscovery in itself was accidental, for Bingham was not looking for Machu Picchu at all. He had mounted his expedition in the mistaken belief that he would find Vilcabanba, the last Inca city to have fallen to the Spanish *conquistadores*, in the valley, but what he discovered more than made up for his disappointment. Here, in the heart of a deep Andean valley, he came across the heavily overgrown ruins of an almost perfectly preserved and hitherto unknown Inca site.

Machu Picchu's story is bound up with the

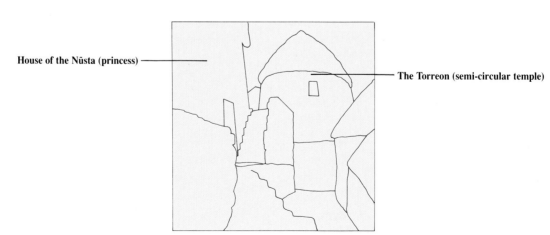

House of the Nũsta (princess) —————

————— The Torreon (semi-circular temple)

SACRIFICES TO THE SUN

Inti, the Sun God, was the chief deity of the Inca pantheon; the other important ones were Illapa, the god of the storm and the thunderbolt, and Mama Quilla, the moon goddess. The most important festivals took place at the times of the mid-summer and mid-winter solstices. Evidence from Cuzco indicates that these ceremonies lasted for eight days, the high point being the ritual sacrifice of animals, ranging from llamas to sheep, to Inti.

Animals were slaughtered on the sacred altar — the one at Machu Picchu (center left) was known as the Hitching Post of the Sun, access to which was gained via a flight of stone steps (far left).

The gold sacrificial knife used in such religious ceremonies was known as a tumi *(left). This example comes from an Inca center on the northern coast of Peru and dates from between 1300 and 1466.*

career of the great Inca ruler Pachacuti, who conquered this jungle wilderness in around AD1438. He subsequently drove a road up the valley of the Vilcanota, where he founded a series of new settlements. The road ended at Machu Picchu, some 62 miles (100 kilometers) north of the Inca capital at Cuzco.

Why was it built?

Here, the mystery starts. No one really knows what inspired Pachacuti to build in this inaccessible and inhospitable spot, with its wet and miserable weather, though some plausible explanations have been put forward. Early researchers believed that Machu Picchu was yet another Inca city, but its size — with its 200 or so buildings, it could have housed little more than 1,000 people — counts against this view. What is clear is that the high quality of masonry construction and the absence of poorer quality buildings here means that Machu Picchu was no ordinary settlement.

Based on this, some archaeologists have suggested that Machu Picchu was intended as a fortified frontier citadel. There was certainly a defensive aspect to the site. Its more vulnerable approaches were defended by a dry moat and by walls, pierced with narrow gates, while look-out posts and signal stations were located on the surrounding hills. However, the argument is difficult to sustain, for the fortifications were left incomplete and the walls were poorly designed to resist concerted attack.

A religious sanctuary

What now seems far more likely is that Machu Picchu was a religious sanctuary, consisting of a cluster of holy buildings enclosed by a precinct wall, which served to delineate the sacred area and exclude the profane. Above all, it served as a potent symbol of Inca power in

The drawings here come from contemporary Inca records and provide a vivid insight into everyday life. The young girl (top left) is aged between 14 and 20. She is a sipas or tasqui sipas from the conquered provinces, rather than a true Inca. She carries her distaff and pachca *(spindle). The picture (bottom left) is a scene from the investiture of Huascar, the last Inca emperor, in 1525, together with that of his sister, Chuqui Huipa, as his empress. Above, Inca* nŭstas, *the name given to pure-born Inca girls, are seen bathing.*

what was a newly conquered territory.

There is substantial archaeological evidence to support this point of view, for the site contains a remarkable number of shrines. Some were in caves, while others were formed from rocky outcrops, called *huaca*. The most important, or at least the most impressively built, were arranged around the small square known as the sacred Plaza, on the west side of the city. From one end of this square, a steep processional way — with vertical drops to the river far below — wound up to a sculpted stone outcrop higher up the mountain. This was the *inti-hautana*. It has been suggested that this was a solar observatory, where the equinox could have been measured from the shadow of a stone column at the center of the shrine. Here, too, the midsummer and midwinter sun festivals would have been held.

Festivals, sacrifices and the *Mamacunas*

The sacrifices and ceremonies the celebration of these festivals entailed lasted for eight days at a time, according to the evidence we have from the Inca capital of Cuzco. From sunrise to sunset, the Inca priests and lords, all dressed in their finest robes, maintained a constant chant, thanking the Sun God for favoring them with past good harvests and praying for equal fortune with the next. Throughout the day, too, sacrificial offerings were burnt on a great fire. There were no human sacrifices, however. Lambs were considered to be the most sacred offering, though rabbits, birds, tallow, crops and vegetables are also known to have been thought worthy of sacrifice.

The Sun God was also served by a band of carefully chosen women priestesses — the *Mamacunas*. These were selected for their noble birth or their beauty before they reached the age of eight. From that time, they lived in secluded communities, where their chastity was strictly guarded. Their main occupations were the weaving of intricate textiles for priestly garments and the brewing of special maize beer for the Inca festivals. Certainly, it is clear that women played an important part in the society of Machu Picchu; four out of five of all the skeletons that have been discovered in the burial caves around the site are female and their graves are also the most richly furnished.

The Torreon

Another central feature of Machu Picchu is the Torreon, so-called because it was once thought to be a defensive tower, though it may also have been a sun temple. The unusual curved wall of the building surrounded a sacred rock outcrop, which the Incas carved into an altar. The grotto below the rock is known as the royal mausoleum. Niches carved into its sides were of the appropriate size to have housed the royal mummies, though there is no direct evidence that they actually did so. To the left of the Torreon is the House of the Nūsta. Some archaeologists have identified this as the home of the high priest or priestess, but it could equally well have been a temple dedicated to some of the lesser celestial gods.

The main residential areas were spread along the terraces of the northern and southern parts of the site. The homes here were typically simple stone buildings, with thatch roofs. Inside, they were gloomy, undecorated and scantily furnished. There were no chairs or beds, for instance; the Incas probably slept in their clothes on mats laid over the floor. The houses were arranged in groups of between two and eight, built around courtyards where most domestic activities, including cooking and weaving, took place.

An abandoned city

Though the facts behind the creation of Machu Picchu are obscure, the reasons for its speedy abandonment are less of a mystery. Once Inca power had crumbled in the face of speedy conquest by the Spanish *conquistadores*, the reasoning that had sustained the existence of Machu Picchu similar ceased to exist. The site was simply abandoned by its people and the jungle returned – until the momentous rediscovery early this century.

Macchu Picchu's Torreon was either a defensive tower or a sun temple, the later now being considered the more likely. It was built over a sacred grotto known as the royal mausoleum. The niches carved in its stone walls may well have housed the royal mummies, carried in stately procession through the gateway (below). Ritual and religion were an integral part of Inca daily life. For them, their emperor was divine — he was the son of Inti, the Sun God — and still watched over his people in the afterlife. His mummified corpse was therefore an object of veneration; it was part of Inca religious ritual, for instance, to take the mummified king on a processional tour of the lands he had once ruled.

PROCESSIONS, GOD-KINGS AND THE AFTERLIFE

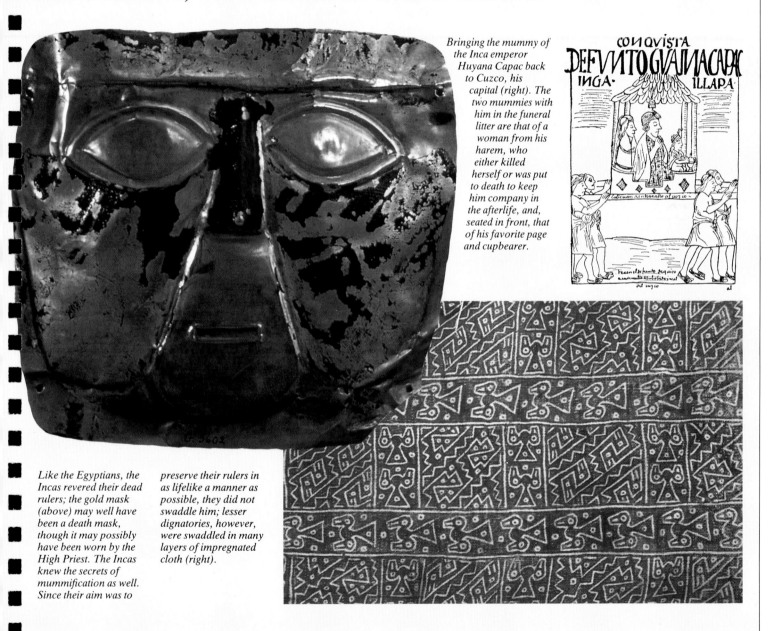

Bringing the mummy of the Inca emperor Huyana Capac back to Cuzco, his capital (right). The two mummies with him in the funeral litter are that of a woman from his harem, who either killed herself or was put to death to keep him company in the afterlife, and, seated in front, that of his favorite page and cupbearer.

Like the Egyptians, the Incas revered their dead rulers; the gold mask (above) may well have been a death mask, though it may possibly have been worn by the High Priest. The Incas knew the secrets of mummification as well. Since their aim was to preserve their rulers in as lifelike a manner as possible, they did not swaddle him; lesser dignatories, however, were swaddled in many layers of impregnated cloth (right).

THE BAYON – ANGKOR THOM

*A fabulous religious monument stands at the heart of a complex of "capitals",
which lay lost and forgotten in the Cambodian jungle for some 400 years*

Deep in the Cambodian jungle lie the ruins of Angkor. Once the capital of the Khmer empire, Angkor was lost and forgotten for some 400 years, during which time the jungle gradually came back into its own. Then, in 1860, the French natural historian Henri Mouhot fortuitously came across its heavily overgrown remains.

How old is Angkor and how did it come into existence? Inscriptions on the site make it clear that the kings who reigned here claimed descent from Jayavarman II. He held power in the late 8th and early 9th centuries. He was a key figure in this period of Cambodian history and seems to have done much to unite the various kingdoms and principates into which 8th-century Cambodia was divided, albeit by force of arms. However Jayavarman II did not build at Angkor.

The first Khmer ruler to set up his capital here was Yasovarman, who came to the throne in AD889. Apart from a brief interval between

Henri Mouhot drew this sketch map (below) to show his approach to Angkor from his disembarkation point on the Siem Reap river.

The eastern entrance pavilion, surmounted by a tower at Preah Palilay (below). Mouhot wrote that everywhere was "intermingled with large trees, creepers and thistles, which invade the courts, the terraces and other parts."

Central complex of towers

Roofs of third floor

Entrances

Porch

Entrances

Roofs of third floor

Porch

921 and 940, the Khmer kings kept their capitals here until the final abandonment of the site in 1431.

Angkor — the name is derived from the Sanskrit for "city" or "capital" — was not so much a town as a series of religious and administrative enclaves. The reason for their emergence was simple. Each successive king, assuming he held office long enough to do so, built himself a completely new capital at Angkor until some time in the 13th century. In all, some 50 of these separate sites have been discovered, their layout being broadly the same in each instance.

Centered on temples

Each Khmer capital was arranged around a main temple, where the state religion was established. Today, Angkor is still completely dominated by the ruins of these buildings. One reason for their survival is simple — according to Khmer religious beliefs, only the gods were entitled to buildings of stone. All of the non-religious structures, even including the royal palaces, were built of wood and so have long since vanished.

Khmer culture and religion was deeply influenced by those of India, and, in the earlier capitals, the state temples were usually, although not always, dedicated to the Hindu god Shiva. They were set on top of stepped pyramids, which symbolized the god's sacred mountain home. Each capital had its own temple-mountain, which, in most cases, housed a sacred carved stone phallus, known as a *linga*. On this, the names of the god and the reigning king were inscribed in a combined form — the combination not only represented the life-giving force of Shiva himself, but also seems to have been a potent symbol of the power of kingship. Though archaeologists are

As Angkor expanded from around AD900 onward, ruler after ruler made his own contribution to the site. As temple followed temple, so, too, did a network of canals, dikes, moats and two massive reservoirs called baray, on the eastern and western sides of the complex respectively. In all 72 major monuments survive — they are all religious structures, since everything else, including the royal palaces, was built of wood, rather than stone. Their sheer scale was not realized until aerial surveys were made; the examples here (left, below) come from an RAF photographic over-flight, made in 1946.

THE MASTER-BUILDERS OF ANGKOR

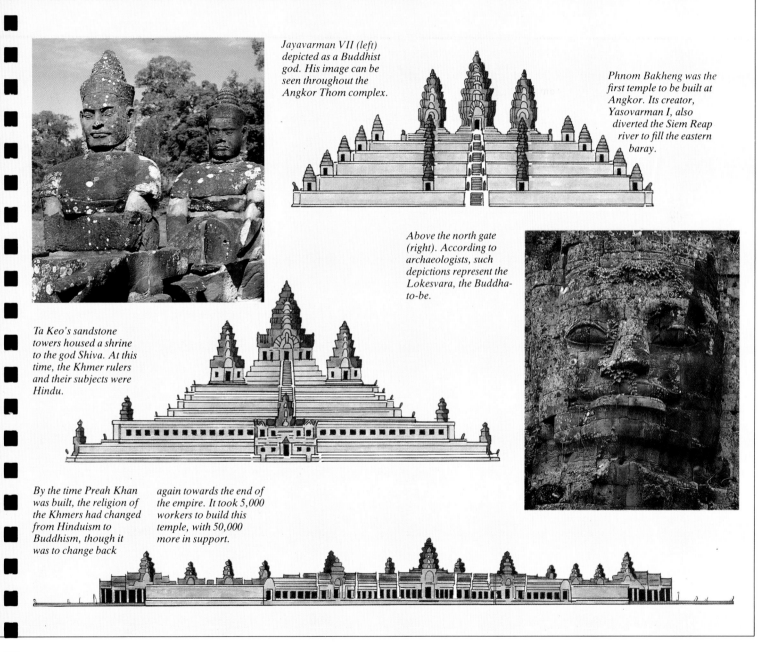

Jayavarman VII (left) depicted as a Buddhist god. His image can be seen throughout the Angkor Thom complex.

Phnom Bakheng was the first temple to be built at Angkor. Its creator, Yasovarman I, also diverted the Siem Reap river to fill the eastern baray.

Above the north gate (right). According to archaeologists, such depictions represent the Lokesvara, the Buddha-to-be.

Ta Keo's sandstone towers housed a shrine to the god Shiva. At this time, the Khmer rulers and their subjects were Hindu.

By the time Preah Khan was built, the religion of the Khmers had changed from Hinduism to Buddhism, though it was to change back again towards the end of the empire. It took 5,000 workers to build this temple, with 50,000 more in support.

The elaborately carved door frame in the sanctuary, Ta Prohm. Stone for all the buildings of the Angkor came from the Phnom Kulen range of mountains, some 20 miles (32 kilometers) to the northwest.

still uncertain as to whether the Khmer rulers were considered to be god-kings, there is no doubt that they held sacred power, which was manifested in these temples.

Several temples were left unfinished, while others show signs of having being completed in a hurry, because work on them probably came to a stop when a king died, the builders being diverted to start the building of his successor's capital. While a king lived, his temple formed the center of the Khmer cosmos; on his death, it served as a funerary temple, where the king was venerated under a new name.

The beauty of the Bayon

The most celebrated of these temple cities are Angkor Wat and Angkor Thom. Angkor Wat, the earlier of the two, is perhaps the most perfect of the mountain-temple sites — it is probably the largest religious structure in the world — but the Bayon, which lies at the heart of Angkor Thom, is unquestionably one of the world's strangest and most fabulous single monuments. It lies at the heart of a vast precinct enclosed by both a perimeter wall nearly two miles (3.2 meters) long and a moat crossed by five bridges.

The Bayon is more sculpture than structure. It is dominated by the serene smiles of the many carved four-sided faces, each some 23 feet (seven meters) high, that adorn its towers

and gates. These images, facing the four points of the compass, were perhaps intended to represent the Bodhisvatta Lokesvara, whose compassionate, all-seeing gaze offered universal salvation. It seems likely, too, that the faces were also modeled on that of Jayavarman VII, the king who built the temple.

Jayavarman, crowned in 1181, was one of the greatest of the Khmer kings. He was a successful warrior — his naval victory over the rival Chams is depicted on reliefs inside the Bayon – and under his rule the Khmer empire reached its greatest territorial extent. Khmer power extended as far afield as Burma and the South China Sea, while the rulers of Java and Vietnam both paid Jayavarman tribute. He was a great builder, too; inscriptions show him to have been responsible for the building of temples, roads, rest houses (referred to as "the houses with a fire") and hospitals throughout the kingdom.

Jayavarman was also a Buddhist — Buddhism was gradually to replace Hinduism as the dominant religion across most of Indochina — and the central tower of the Bayon accordingly bears a giant image of Buddha. Surrounding the tower is a forest of more than 50 smaller ones, each studded with multiple heads of the king, depicted as a Buddhist god. However, other religions were also tolerated here; shrines dedicated to Vishna and Shiva, as well as to past Khmer rulers, were set in the many smaller chapels within the complex.

Life at Angkor Thom

Despite the detailed reliefs that adorn the Bayon, which include scenes from everyday life, we know little about how the people of Angkor Thom actually lived. Undoubtedly, temple life was dominated by priestly and royal elites, who would have called on the services of

A RECORD OF EVERYDAY LIFE

The majority of the vivid reliefs decorating the Bayon record the achievements of Jayavarman VII, but the bottom band consists of a lively sequence of scenes from everyday life. Though originally intended to provide a context of time and place for the main compositions, today they give a rare and fascinating glimpse into the way in which the ordinary people of this lost civilization lived.

Dinner is prepared for the king and his companions (above left), while a relief showing a man and his ox-cart (above) reveals how little peasant life has changed over the centuries. Similar carts are still in use today.

Dancing asparas (top) were important in Khmer religion; elephants, too, were a common and potent symbol, as the Terrace of the Elephants demonstrates (left).

a large servile population. This view is confirmed by an inscription from Ta Prohm, a temple complex built some years before the Bayon. It reads: "Here are 400 men, 18 great priests, 2,740 officials, 2,223 assistants including 615 dancing girls. Altogether 12,640 including those entitled to lodgings."

Further valuable evidence comes from Chinese sources. Chou Ta-kuan, an envoy from Peking to the Khmer court, described the Bayon, with its golden central tower flanked by more than 20 stone ones, as he found it toward the end of the 13th century. By this time it was no longer held necessary for each new king to build his own capital. Consequently Angkor Thom remained in continued use, though later rulers converted the Bayon into a temple for Shiva.

Angkor abandoned

Some time after the reign of Jayavarman VII, the Khmer empire went into decline. The period of imperial growth had encouraged the development of a series of complex social, economic and administrative institutions. In particular, an extremely high level of agricultural productivity had been achieved, but this depended on the maintenance of complex irrigation and drainage systems.

Herein lay the seeds of ultimate failure. These systems proved highly vulnerable to any form of recession or crisis, as events in the early 14th century were to show. Not only did the Cham manage to free themselves from their Khmer masters; as Chou Ta-Kuan recorded, the empire also had to face two invasions from neighboring Thailand. In 1431, the Thais sacked and occupied Angkor. The Khmers fled south, leaving their abandoned capital at the mercy of the jungle and their empire in ruins. It was never to re-emerge.

MOHENJO-DARO

Hill-top center of a 4,000-year old civilization that flourished along the Indus Valley

Today, it is difficult to imagine that the semidesert arid scrubland of the Indus Valley was once the center of one of the world's major Bronze Age civilizations. Modern archaeology, however, has revealed that this was indeed the case. Excavations at Mohenjo-Daro confirm that here, at the beginning of the second millenium BC, some 4000 years ago, cities fit to rival the greatest urban centers of contemporary Egypt and Mesopotamia stood and flourished.

This civilization, which covered most of present-day Pakistan as well as a considerable stretch of the northwest Indian coast, was ruled from two great cities — Harappa, rediscovered in 1921, and the better preserved Mohenjo-Daro, found the following year. What archaeologists discovered at both sites were great *tells*, immense mounds formed by the leveled remains of many phases of building superimposed one over the other.

Mohenjo-Daro covers a vast circular area, up to five miles (9.6 kilometers) in circumference. In places, the house platforms rise some 40 feet (12.1 meters) above the Indus flood plain, but some of the earliest remains are buried beneath the level of the modern water

Mohanjo-Daro, midway up the Indus Valley, was one of the two key centers of the Indus civilization. The other, Harappa, was further upstream (below). Both were the home of skilled craftsmen; these attractive carved dice (inset) come from Mohanjo-Daro.

Mohenjo-Daro stretches over a large circular area, rising towards a central citadel. Here you can see the stupa in the background. The reconstruction (right) shows one of the streets of the citadel, looking towards the Great Bath.

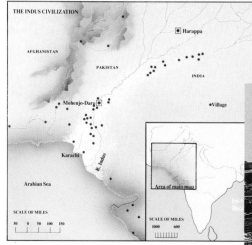

THE INDUS CIVILIZATION

AFGHANISTAN

PAKISTAN

Harappa

INDIA

Mohenjo-Daro

•Village

Karachi

R. Indus

Arabian Sea

Area of main map

SCALE OF MILES
50 0 50 100 150

SCALE OF MILES
1000 600

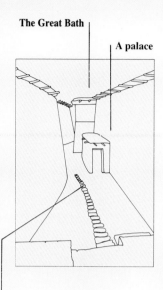

The Great Bath

A palace

Central main drainage channel
concealed beneath layer of stones

A bust of a priest (below), found in the area of the lower town. It is made of glazed steatite, the slit eyes being inlaid with shell.

A model two-wheel ox-cart, with its two ox bullocks (below). Such carts, with their solid wheels, were the commonest form of land transport. They are not unlike those still in use in modern Sind. The Great Bath (bottom) is seen from the air. Water and cleanliness were extremely important to the city's inhabitants.

This figure of a woman (above) is made of terracotta. She is thought to be votive — that is, created as a religious offering.

potential threat, particularly during the time of the monsoon.

Two unusual buildings stood on the summit. The first of these, the Great Bath, was a large courtyard building, entered by two flights of stairs, surrounding a brick-lined pool some 39 feet (11.8 meters) long, 23 feet (seven meters) wide and 8 feet (2.4 meters) deep. Just as in modern Hinduism, ceremonial bathing was extremely important to Mohenjo-Daro's inhabitants, so it is reasonable to conclude that the Great Bath played a central part in the religious life of the city, or its rulers. Moreover, evidence from elsewhere on the site confirms that the city's builders were fully aware of the sanitary needs of the population.

Next to the Great Bath stand the brick foundations of another building. Until recently, this was thought to have been a granary, but this interpretation has recently been disputed. In its original form, it measured 150 feet (45.7 meters) by 75 feet (22.5 meters). If, as earlier archaeologists supposed, it was a granary, it is likely that it would have housed the agricultural surplus we know was brought to the city as tribute and tithes. The existence of this surplus would have provided the necessary economic foundations for the growth of a complex urban society. Certainly, some of the surplus would have consisted in the main of wheat and barley, the chief crops harvested in the Indus valley although rice was also grown on a few Harappan sites. Other buildings may have included temples, audience halls and palaces.

table and it is consequently difficult to study them in detail. Enough has been found, however, to date the site's initial occupation. This had certainly taken place by about 2500BC.

A man-made hill

The principal buildings of the city were set high on an artificial mound, built of mud bricks and surrounded by a deep moat. This man-made hill, approximately 400 to 500 yards (365 to 457 meters) long and 200 to 300 yards (182.8 to 274 meters) wide, is known as the citadel or acropolis. Solid brick towers and walls built around the hill perhaps served as defenses, though it is thought that the city was in greater need of protection from floods than from human enemies. The Indus was always a

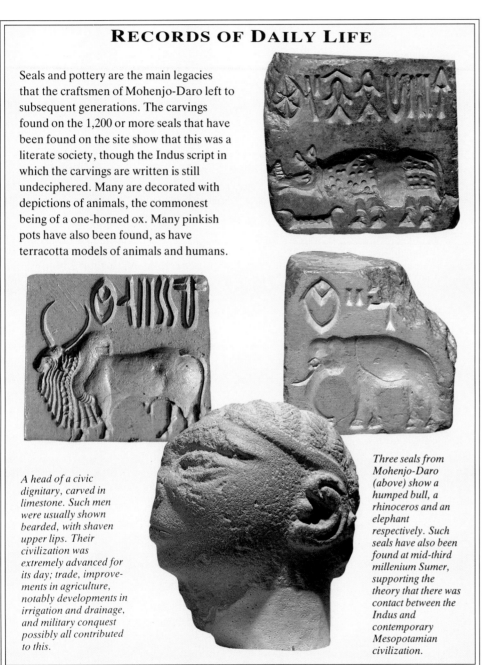

RECORDS OF DAILY LIFE

Seals and pottery are the main legacies that the craftsmen of Mohenjo-Daro left to subsequent generations. The carvings found on the 1,200 or more seals that have been found on the site show that this was a literate society, though the Indus script in which the carvings are written is still undeciphered. Many are decorated with depictions of animals, the commonest being of a one-horned ox. Many pinkish pots have also been found, as have terracotta models of animals and humans.

A head of a civic dignitary, carved in limestone. Such men were usually shown bearded, with shaven upper lips. Their civilization was extremely advanced for its day; trade, improvements in agriculture, notably developments in irrigation and drainage, and military conquest possibly all contributed to this.

Three seals from Mohenjo-Daro (above) show a humped bull, a rhinoceros and an elephant respectively. Such seals have also been found at mid-third millenium Sumer, supporting the theory that there was contact between the Indus and contemporary Mesopotamian civilization.

Beneath the citadel

The streets of the lower city were laid out on a grid pattern. They were crowded with flat-roofed brick houses, with austere and even monotonous blank facades facing directly out on to the dusty, unpaved streets. There were few windows, while even the front doors were concealed down narrow alleyways.

Household life centered on the open courts, around which the rooms were arranged. Some houses had upper floors, while latrines have been found in several buildings. One of Mohenjo-Daro's striking features is the close attention its inhabitants paid to personal hygiene. Houses were equipped with elaborate brick-floored bathrooms, while it has been estimated that the city contained over 700 wells, despite the proximity of the river.

On the outskirts of town were the crafts-men's quarters, with workshops and a huddle of smaller houses. Nearer to the town center, the houses were larger and more spacious – it is possible that some of them also contained accommodation for domestic slaves. From this evidence, it has been estimated that the city may have had a population of around 40,000 when the civilization was at its height.

Victim of nature

There was a marked deterioration in civic standards during the later phases of occupation, though the reasons for it are unclear. Parts of the city seem to have been abandoned, leaving empty areas where bodies had been flung into the street or carelessly dumped into shallow pits.

By the end of the 19th century BC, however, it seems that the city had lost its age-old battle with the elements. The intermittent recurrence of destructive floods may have been a key factor in hastening the fall of this civilization.

GREAT ZIMBABWE

Massive, superbly crafted walls of stone still stand around the site of the city that Shona built to form the hub of their empire.

Pottery models of humped cattle (below), found in the ruins of Great Zimbabwe. Cattle were very important to the Shona; they played a major part in Shona urbanization and subsequent prosperity.

One of the soapstone birds (below) found in the eastern enclosure in the last years of the 19th century. Its design encouraged the view that Zimbabwe had not been built by black Africans.

With its massive, superbly crafted stone walls, Great Zimbabwe is undoubtedly the most dramatic archaeological site in sub-Saharan Africa. Small wonder, then, that tales of its grandeur — even in its ruined state — surprised and mystified the first European explorers to hear about the site. This was in the 16th century, though Great Zimbabwe itself was not physically rediscovered until around 1870.

An African empire

It is now known that Great Zimbabwe was the capital of a Shona-speaking empire that flourished between the 13th and 15th centuries AD. This empire covered most of the present-day state of Zimbabwe, as well as parts of Botswana, the northern Transvaal and Mozambique. The city itself is likely to have housed a population in excess of 10,000.

The origins of this empire date back some 1500 years to the time when stable agricultural societies, with permanent village settlements and complex social organization, were becoming established in this part of Africa. The later emergence of an urban soci-

The Great Enclosure (left), viewed from the Acropolis. The outer wall is the largest single prehistoric structure in sub-Saharan Africa. More stonework was used in its building than in the rest of Great Zimbabwe put together.

Dentelle-patterned frieze

Conical tower

Wall of the Great Enclosure

Bands of dark aphibolite

Decorations on bands of dark aphibolite

Daga plaster

Stepped platform

Daga plaster

Monoliths

Daga platform

As such large-scale building work required a considerable degree of planning, Shona society was clearly highly organized. The site is dominated by the Hill Ruins, also known as the Acropolis, where there are the remains of two massive enclosures. The one to the west probably contained the royal palace. This, in common with other residential enclosures, consisted of a series of huts, with red or yellow clay walls and grass roofs. As well as the king's living quarters, the palace also contained an audience chamber.

The eastern enclosure lay behind the royal residence. It was probably used for ceremonial activities — the Shona treat the area in front of buildings as profane and public and that behind them as private and sacred. This theory is born out by the important ceremonial artefacts that have been discovered in this enclosure — not to mention a series of intriguing objects carved in soapstone. These included four birds on top of carved monoliths, other monoliths decorated with geometric motifs and a large number of small carved cylinders, resembling phalli.

Within the enclosure, too, there is an underground passage. This is where the king called on the spirits of his ancestors to intercede with the Shona supreme god on behalf of the nation.

Shards of pottery (above) and the iron spoon (below) bear witness to the extent of Shona prosperity.

Both were imported, the spoon probably coming from the East African coast.

ety is likely to have been influenced by several factors, as was the rise of Great Zimbabwe itself to become the most powerful of the cities the Shona created. The site itself had a number of natural advantages. It lay in fertile, well-watered and lightly-wooded hill country, astride some of the most important trade routes that linked the inland gold-producing areas with the coast. The region was also well endowed with natural building materials — weathered large rectangular blocks of granite from the hills surrounding the site were perfect for use in massive stone constructions. The thick walls of Great Zimbabwe were the first fruits of this ready availability; they were not built as defences, but to demonstrate the importance of the city and its ruler.

The mystery of the Great Enclosure

At the foot of the hill was an open area. This was the men's court, where political meetings and trials were held. To the south stood a large walled enclosure, which is likely to have been occupied by the king's wives. For the Shona, wives were an important status symbol and it has been estimated that some 300 lived here. They were placed under the tutelage of the king's first wife, who was also responsible for

GROWTH, TRADE AND PROSPERITY

Several factors led to the emergence of the Shona empire and the founding of Great Zimbabwe. For the Shona, cattle meant power, which became centralized under a single ruler; cattle also meant wealth. Both encouraged the emergence of ruling elites and consequently cities, built around royal courts from where administrative, economic and religious affairs could be directed. Control of trade was a further factor in the success of such sites.

Fragments of drawn copper or bronze wire, coiled around a solid core to form ornamental anklets and bracelets (top).

Iron hoes (center), found in the Renders ruin.

Iron pincers and a drawplate (bottom), the latter pierced to take the extruded metal.

Contrast the ruins of the royal treasury (top right) with the reconstruction (right). Walls, steps, seats, pot stands, fireplaces, post collars and edgings were all molded in daga.

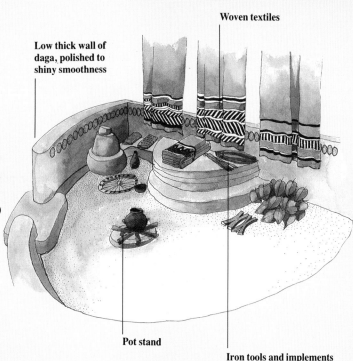

Woven textiles

Low thick wall of daga, polished to shiny smoothness

Pot stand

Iron tools and implements

royal property. One hut in the enclosure contained a royal treasury and this is likely to have been her home.

The most puzzling remains at Great Zimbabwe, however, are those of the Great Enclosure, with its conical inner tower. The enclosure was surrounded by a massive wall up to 36 feet (10.9 meters) high, which was built of some 900,000 stone blocks and decorated with a chevron frieze. Though it has been widely argued that the enclosure was a royal court or religious center, the more convincing suggestion is that it was a place of initiation for adolescents approaching adulthood. Passages linked the enclosure directly to both the wive's enclosure and the men's court, while symbols within it are tokens of masculinity and femininity — men being represented by monoliths and women by grooves — as well as of the sacred and profane. These are carefully set in a series of spaces suitable for use in the initiation rites documented in similar African societies. Finds here also included a large variety of figurines, which elsewhere are associated with girls' initiation schools.

The city's other houses consisted of groups of huts, with accommodation for wives, children and guests, all set around courtyards, which were the base of daily life. The city's economy was based on cattle, trade and cottage industries, such as the making of pottery. A fair amount of time was also dedicated to the brewing and drinking of beer.

From prosperity to decline

Great Zimbabwe was at its most prosperous in the early 15th century, but, as alternative trade centers grew in importance, it went into gradual decline. By the end of the century, building there had ceased and the site was eventually abandoned, until its 19th century rediscovery.

PICTURE CREDITS

l = left; r = right; c = centre; t = top; b = bottom